# THE
# HUNGRY
# STUDENT
# VEGAN
## COOKBOOK

MORE THAN **200** DELICIOUS AND
NUTRITIOUS VEGAN RECIPES

spruce

SOY TOFU SALAD WITH CORIANDER

MUSHROOM STROGANOFF

An Hachette UK Company
www.hachette.co.uk

First published in Great Britain in 2018 by Spruce,
a division of Octopus Publishing Group Ltd,
Carmelite House, 50 Victoria Embankment
London EC4Y 0DZ
www.octopusbooks.co.uk

ISBN 978-1-84601-549-6

A CIP catalogue record for this book is available
from the British Library

Printed and bound in China

10 9 8 7 6 5 4 3 2 1

Standard level spoon measurement are used
in all recipes.
1 tablespoon = one 15 ml spoon
1 teaspoon = one 5 ml spoon

Both imperial and metric measurements have been
given in all recipes. Use one set of measurements only
and not a mixture of both.

Ovens should be preheated to the specific temperature
– if using a fan-assisted oven, follow manufacturer's
instructions for adjusting the time and the temperature.

Pepper should be freshly ground black pepper unless
otherwise stated.

Check the label on all ingredients to ensure they are
suitable for vegans.

RAW CHERRY & ALMOND CAKE
WITH CHOCOLATE GANACHE

# CONTENTS

# INTRODUCTION

Moving away from home is both an exciting and an uncertain time. You're about to embark on the next stage of your life – and the first one that involves fending for yourself. From working out how to operate complex appliances such as the washing machine, to setting your own alarm clock, doing your own grocery shopping and giving up the luxury of the mum and dad taxi service, going to college is a steep learning curve...and that's before you've even started the learning part!

For the first few days or weeks, food is probably not the highest entry on your list of priorities – you eat when you're hungry and as long as it's palatable and fills you up, it's fine. But there will come a point when you crave a meal that doesn't involve putting a random ingredient between two slices of bread, or scraping the contents of a can into a bowl and watching it turn sadly inside a microwave. And that's when you'll unpack this book from the box under your bed and flick through to find the makings of a decent dinner.

Luckily, you don't need to be an accomplished chef to prepare any of the recipes over the following pages. You presumably have a certain amount of common sense and intelligence or you wouldn't be going to college – and that's pretty much all you'll need to cook, bake and grill yourself to foodie heaven. As a vegan student, you've no doubt come across all the stereotypes imaginable, but there's absolutely no reason why you can't eat well and healthily while sticking to a budget. With a little forward planning, a few key utensils and a well-stocked fridge and storecupboard, you can enjoy homemade meals every day, with plenty of delicious snacks and treats thrown in for good measure.

# PLANNING AND BUDGETING

Before you arrive in your new digs, it's a good idea to have a conversation with your housemates about how the grocery shopping and cooking is going to work. Are you going to shop together as a household or each buy your own food? Are you going to take turns cooking or just decide on the day and cook for whoever is at home?

Food that goes missing from the fridge and people who owe money for shopping are issues that can quickly escalate into major disputes. Not everyone has the same ideas about communal shopping and cooking and, while most people are happy to pull their weight and contribute time, money and a bit of effort into stocking up the cupboards, preparing meals and clearing up afterwards, it's not a given. If everyone agrees to a few basic house rules before you move in, there's less chance of people falling out when someone drinks the soya milk by mistake, or if after a night in the pub someone helps themselves to the ingredients you've bought for a special dinner.

If you're going to buy groceries as a household, online shopping is a good solution as it means that you don't all have to physically trudge to the supermarket on a weekly basis – you can shop from home and take your time to work out the best deals and the most convenient delivery time. Order all your basics together so the bill can be split evenly. The same applies when it comes to cooking: choose some easy midweek meals and share the cooking. But when it comes to ordering specialist ingredients, or an item that only one person wants, it's best to do this separately.

# BUDGETING CHECKLIST:

- Make a weekly meal plan. Obviously this won't be set in stone, as plans change and not everyone will be at home every night. But a simple plan means that you only order the food you need, and nothing get wasted.
- Agree a total amount that you feel happy spending on food each week. If you're shopping together, take into account that not everyone will have the same budget or priorities.
- Once a month, buy things like toilet roll, breakfast cereal, cleaning products and canned goods in bulk – as you'll generally save money by buying these groceries in bigger quantities.
- You don't have to just shop in one supermarket – become savings savvy by using comparison sites to find the best deals.
- Some supermarkets offer delivery deals – you pay an annual fee and get free, unlimited delivery slots.
- If there's an incredible offer on a certain ingredient, swap your recipe plan – flexibility is key.

# ESSENTIAL EQUIPMENT

You don't need a kitchen fit for a photo shoot, or kitted out like a professional restaurant, in order to rustle up a decent meal. In fact, it's better to keep things simple – stick to essential utensils and implements so you don't clutter up cupboards and end up with more washing up than needs to be done. Here's a list of the basics that will see you through every recipe in the book.

## Utensils

- Measuring jug
- Measuring spoons
- Mixing bowls (1 small, 1 large)
- Wooden spoons × 2
- Rolling pin
- Grater
- Spatula
- Chopping boards
- Vegetable peeler
- Whisk
- Sharp knives × 2 (1 small, 1 large)

## Pots and pans

- Saucepans × 3 (large, medium and small, with lids)
- Frying pan
- Colander (metal so it can also be used as a steamer)

## Cookware

- Metal baking trays
- Wire cooling rack
- Ovenproof dishes
- Casserole dish
- Muffin tray
- Loaf tin
- Toaster

# Staying healthy

Leaving home and fending for yourself can come as a bit of a shock to the system. As well as navigating a new town or city, finding your way around campus and taking charge of your own washing, cooking and cleaning, it's also important to look after your health. Late, boozy nights and long days studying (yes, you need to do that too!) don't always leave a lot of time to plan for healthy meals and exercise. But your body and brain will only function well if you eat a balanced diet and take regular exercise. Halls of residence and shared student houses are also breeding grounds for germs so anything you can do to boost your immune system will help you to fight off any winter colds or bouts of flu that are doing the rounds.

**Eat your greens** – forget five a day, try and eat up to ten portions of fresh fruit and vegetables every day, in order to stay in tip-top condition. Snack on fruit during the day, add salad to your lunch and steam plenty of fresh vegetables for dinner.

**Run riot** – you don't need to join a gym or pay for expensive fitness classes to keep in shape. You can take up running, work out at home or offer your services as a dog walker (and earn a bit of cash in the process) to make sure you get regular exercise.

**Steer clear of colds** – easier said than done but if you see your housemates dropping like flies from some nasty virus or the dreaded flu, consider escaping back home for a couple of days until the contagious period has passed.

**Clean it up** – students are not generally known for their high standards of hygiene in the kitchen. And while you might be a stickler for a disinfected surface, your housemates and visiting friends might not be as worried about germs clustering on dirty dishcloths and colonies of bacteria growing in unwashed tea mugs. Wash cloths and tea towels regularly, wipe down surfaces with disinfectant and use antiseptic hand wash.

**Food hygiene** - as a vegan, you'll avoid a number of obvious food-related issues in the kitchen but there are still plenty of ways to make yourself ill if you're not careful, and a dodgy salad leaf can harbour just as many potential bugs as a piece of chicken. Always fully defrost food before using it; do not reheat cooked food more than once (and check that it is piping hot all the way through); consume food by the use-by date; and put any leftovers in the fridge or freezer as soon as they're cool enough to transfer.

# THE VEGAN STORECUPBOARD

Whether you have a shelf or a whole cupboard to store your food, there are certain ingredients that you should always keep in stock. You can buy many of these ingredients in bulk and save money - as long as you have the space to store them. But fresh fruit, vegetables, tofu and meat and cheese replacements should be bought often and in smaller amounts, so you don't waste food.

**Oil** - olive, sunflower, rapeseed or coconut oil are all good options as you can use them in a wide range of dishes.

**Onions and garlic** - you'll use these often so keep a good stock in a cool, dry place. For emergencies, garlic paste is a pretty good substitute for fresh garlic and doesn't require peeling and chopping.

**Tofu** - store fresh tofu in the fridge, where it will keep for 3-5 days.

**Nuts and seeds** - from cashew nuts in stir-fry and curry dishes, to pistachios and pumpkin seeds for healthy daytime snacks, aim to keep a good selection of nuts and seeds in your cupboard.

**Pasta** - egg-free lasagne, spaghetti, penne and macaroni are good staples to have on permanent standby.

**Noodles** - egg-free noodles make a really quick and easy stir-fry dinner. Choose from dry or straight-to-wok varieties, both of which have long shelf lives.

**Rice** - wholegrain is more nutritious but basmati is delicious served with curries, and risotto rice is essential for an Italian supper.

**Grains** - couscous, bulgar wheat, quinoa and polenta are all hearty grains that will make a meal in themselves, or they can be served as a side dish, used in salads or added to soups and stews.

**Pulses** - cans of chickpeas are very handy for curries, as well as lentils (green and red) and split peas for dahl, lasagne, pasta sauces and soups.

**Herbs and spices** - a good selection of dried spices and herbs is the secret to delicious food. Start with chilli, paprika, turmeric, mustard seeds, cumin, coriander, tarragon and oregano. Try to buy fresh herbs, wherever possible, for sauces, salads and garnishes.

**Chopped tomatoes** - cheap and nutritious, these can be used in everything from parmigiana to pizza toppings.

**Coconut milk** - rich and creamy, this is an essential ingredient in many Thai and Indian curries, as well as soups, cakes and desserts.

**Baked beans** - there will be days when nothing but beans on toast will do the trick. Plus, they're great for filling baked potatoes or for adding to a chilli.

# KICK OFF THE DAY

RAW FRESH GINGER & OAT BARS

TOASTED MUESLI
WITH COCONUT CHIPS

MUSHROOM RISOTTO CAKES

FLATBREAD, ROASTED VEG
& HUMMUS

# PEACH & GINGER *Juice*

250 g (8 oz) peaches
2.5 cm (1 inch) piece of fresh root
  ginger, peeled and roughly
  chopped
ice cubes
sparkling mineral water
mint leaves, to serve

Serves **1**
Prep time **10 minutes**

1 Halve the peaches and remove the stones. Juice the peaches with the chopped ginger.

2 Pour the juice into a tall glass over ice, add a splash of sparkling mineral water and a couple of mint leaves and serve immediately.

**VARIATION**
For grapefruit fizz, juice 300 g (10 oz) grapefruit with 350 g (12 oz) cucumber and the juice of ¹/₂ a lemon. Top up with sparkling mineral water and stir in some chopped mint.

AFFORDABILITY 1

# WATERMELON
# & RASPBERRY
# JUICE

about 300 g (10 oz) watermelon
125 g (4 oz) raspberries
2-3 ice cubes

..........................................

Serves **1**
Prep time **10 minutes**

..........................................

1 Halve the melon and deseed. Scoop out the flesh and cut into cubes. Juice the melon with the raspberries.

2 Pour into a glass, add a couple of ice cubes and serve immediately.

**VARIATION**
For watermelon & orange juice, juice 2 oranges with the melon instead of the raspberries.

AFFORDABILITY
**1**

# BEETROOT & BERRY Smoothie

50 g (2 oz) beetroot
100 g (3½ oz) blueberries, plus
  extra to serve (optional)
100 g (3½ oz) raspberries
2–3 ice cubes

Serves **1**
Prep time **10 minutes**

1   Juice the beetroot in a food processor or blender.

2   Add the blueberries, raspberries and ice cubes and process until smooth.

3   Pour the mixture into a glass, decorate with blueberries, if liked, and serve immediately.

AFFORDABILITY **1**

### STUDENT TIP

**SMOOTHIE BOOST** Keep a stock of berries in the freezer for an instant morning smoothie. Combine with non-dairy milk and a handful of oats for a filling breakfast on the go.

# ROASTED GRANOLA

5 tablespoons agave syrup
2 tablespoons sunflower oil
250 g (8 oz) porridge oats
50 g (2 oz) hazelnuts, roughly chopped
50 g (2 oz) blanched almonds, roughly chopped
50 g (2 oz) dried cranberries
50 g (2 oz) dried blueberries

Serves **4**
Prep time **10 minutes,
plus cooling**
Cooking time **25-30 minutes**

1 Heat the agave syrup and oil together gently in a small saucepan.

2 Mix the oats and nuts together thoroughly in a large bowl. Pour over the syrup mixture and stir well to combine.

3 Spread the mixture over a large nonstick baking sheet and bake in a preheated oven, 150°C (300°F), Gas Mark 2, for 20-25 minutes, stirring once, until golden.

4 Leave the granola to cool, then stir in the dried berries. Serve with soya yogurt and fresh fruit. Any remaining granola can be stored in an airtight container.

AFFORDABILITY
1

# RAW FRESH GINGER & OAT BARS

AFFORDABILITY
1

1 Line a cake tin with a base measurement of 22 × 9 cm (8½ × 3½ inch), or a similar-size container, with clingfilm.

2 Put the ginger, tahini and 200 g (7 oz) of the prunes into a food processor and process until smooth.

3 Add the oatmeal, buckwheat and 3 tablespoons of the sesame seeds, and process again until combined. Add the sultanas and pulse briefly.

4 Turn the mixture into the prepared tin and press down firmly in an even layer.

5 Wipe out the processor and process the remaining prunes and the apple juice until you have a very smooth purée.

6 Spread the filling over the oat and buckwheat base and sprinkle with the remaining sesame seeds. Lift out of the tin and serve cut into bars.

5 cm (2 inch) piece of fresh root ginger, grated
2½ tablespoons tahini
300 g (10 oz) pitted prunes
75 g (3 oz) medium oatmeal
75 g (3 oz) buckwheat flakes
4 tablespoons sesame seeds
100 g (3½ oz) sultanas
4 tablespoons apple juice

Makes **16**
Prep time **10 minutes,
  plus soaking**

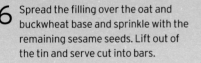

# TOASTED MUESLI
## *with coconut chips*

350 g (12 oz) rolled oats
75 g (3 oz) coconut chips
75 g (3 oz) sunflower seeds
200 g (7 oz) pumpkin seeds
150 g (5 oz) flaked almonds
100 g (3½ oz) hazelnuts
4 tablespoons maple syrup
2 tablespoons sunflower oil
250 g (8 oz) sultanas
75 g (3 oz) dried figs, roughly
   chopped

**To serve**
soya milk
raspberries

Serves **8**
Prep time **15 minutes**
Cooking time **15-20 minutes**

**1** Mix together the oats, coconut chips, sunflower and pumpkin seeds, flaked almonds and hazelnuts in a large bowl.

**2** Transfer half the muesli mixture to a separate bowl. Mix the maple syrup and sunflower oil together in a jug, then pour it over the remaining half of the muesli and toss really well to lightly coat all the ingredients.

**3** Line a large roasting tin with baking paper, scatter over the syrup-coated muesli and spread out in a single layer. Bake in a preheated oven, 150°C (300°F), Gas Mark 2, for 15-20 minutes, stirring occasionally, until golden and crisp.

**4** Leave to cool completely, then toss with the uncooked muesli and the sultanas and figs. Store in an airtight storage jar. Serve with soya milk and raspberries.

**VARIATION**
For soft cinnamon muesli with almonds & banana, mix together 350 g (12 oz) rolled oats, 250 g (8 oz) sultanas, 200 g (7 oz) each pumpkin seeds and toasted blanched almonds, 100 g (3½ oz) soft dried banana slices, 75 g (3 oz) each pitted dried dates and sunflower seeds and 2 teaspoons ground cinnamon in a large bowl. Store in an airtight storage jar. Serve with soya milk or soya yogurt and fresh fruit if liked.

AFFORDABILITY
**1**

# APRICOT & FRESH GINGER MUFFINS

200 g (7 oz) self-raising flour
2 teaspoons baking powder
200 g (7 oz) dried apricots, chopped
100 g (3½ oz) porridge oats, plus extra to sprinkle
125 g (4 oz) caster sugar
finely grated zest and juice of 1 large orange
40 g (1½ oz) fresh root ginger, peeled and finely chopped
100 ml (3½ fl oz) oat milk
100 ml (3½ fl oz) vegetable oil or mild olive oil

Makes **12**
Prep time **10 minutes**
Cooking time **20 minutes**

**1** Line a 12-hole muffin tin with paper muffin cases. Sift the flour and baking powder into a bowl and stir in the apricots, oats and sugar.

**2** In a separate bowl combine the orange zest and juice, ginger, oat milk and oil. Mix well and add to the dry ingredients.

**3** Using a large metal spoon, stir the ingredients together until they're only just combined. Spoon into the muffin cases and sprinkle with extra oats.

**4** Bake in a preheated oven, 200°C (400°F), Gas Mark 6 for 18-20 minutes until the muffins are risen and golden. Serve warm or cold. Any leftover muffins will freeze well – just warm through before serving.

AFFORDABILITY **1**

## STUDENT TIP

**STAY HYDRATED** A busy student life means it's easy to forget to drink enough water. Drink a glass as soon as you get up and keep a bottle in your bag and refill it during the day.

# CARROT & APPLE *Muffins*

1  Line a 12-hole muffin tin with paper cases or lightly oil and line the bases with discs of baking paper.

2  Sift the flour, bicarbonate of soda, salt, cinnamon and ginger together into a bowl. Stir in the raisins, sugar and poppy seeds.

3  Mix the almond milk, oil and vinegar together in a jug. Add to the dry ingredients and lightly stir together until just mixed. Quickly fold in the apple and carrot, then divide the mixture between the paper cases or the holes of the muffin tin.

4  Bake immediately in a preheated oven, 190°C (375°F), Gas Mark 5, for 15-20 minutes until well risen and golden. Transfer to a wire rack to cool. Store the muffins for up to for 2-3 days in an airtight container, or freeze.

300 g (10 oz) self-raising flour
1½ teaspoons bicarbonate of soda
½ teaspoon salt
1½ teaspoons ground cinnamon
1 teaspoon ground ginger
75 g (3 oz) raisins
150 g (5 oz) light muscovado sugar
1 tablespoon poppy seeds
275 ml (9 fl oz) almond milk
100 ml (3½ fl oz) olive oil, plus extra for oiling (optional)
1 tablespoon cider vinegar
1 dessert apple, cored and coarsely grated
1 carrot, peeled and coarsely grated

Makes **12**
Prep time **20 minutes**
Cooking time **15-20 minutes**

AFFORDABILITY 1

# BLUEBERRY & VANILLA
# FRENCH TOAST

1 teaspoon cornflour
75 ml (3 fl oz) oat milk
1 tablespoon caster sugar, plus
   extra for sprinkling
½ teaspoon vanilla extract
2 chunky slices of white or seeded
   vegan bread
1 tablespoon dairy-free spread
1 tablespoon vegetable oil
75 g (3 oz) blueberries
soya yogurt, to serve (optional)

Serves **2**
Prep time **5 minutes**
Cooking time **5 minutes**

1   Put the cornflour in a small bowl and gradually blend in the
    milk until smooth. Add the sugar and vanilla extract and pour
    into a shallow bowl.

2   Turn both bread slices in the flavoured milk until it is evenly
    absorbed.

3   Heat the dairy-free spread and oil in a frying pan until
    bubbling. Fry the bread slices, one at a time if they don't both
    fit, until golden on the underside, about 2 minutes. Turn with
    a fish slice to brown the other side.

4   Transfer to plates and add the blueberries to the pan. Heat
    very briefly to warm through and spoon on to the bread.
    Serve sprinkled with extra sugar and soya yogurt, if liked.

# HOME-BAKED BEANS *on toast*

1 Soak the beans in plenty of cold water overnight. Drain, tip them into a saucepan and cover with cold water.

2 Bring to the boil, then drain and return to the pan. Cover with fresh cold water, bring to the boil and boil for 10 minutes, then cover and simmer for 50 minutes until tender.

3 Meanwhile, heat the oil in a separate saucepan, add the red onion and fry for 3 minutes until just starting to soften.

4 Add the tomatoes, tomato purée, sugar, vinegar, paprika, mustard powder and stock. Bring to the boil, stirring, then reduce the heat and simmer, uncovered, for 20 minutes until reduced slightly.

5 Drain the cooked beans and add to the tomato sauce. Simmer for a further 15-20 minutes, covered, until the sauce has thickened.

6 Season with salt and pepper and serve on wholemeal toast, scattered with the chopped parsley.

350 g (12 oz) dried haricot beans
2 tablespoons rapeseed oil
1 red onion, cut into wedges
400 g (14 oz) can chopped tomatoes
2 tablespoons tomato purée
2 tablespoons dark muscovado sugar
3 tablespoons vegan red wine vinegar
1 teaspoon paprika
1 teaspoon mustard powder
275 ml (9 fl oz) vegetable stock (see page 219)
salt and pepper
2 tablespoons chopped flat leaf parsley, to garnish
wholemeal toast, to serve

Serves **4**
Prep time **10 minutes, plus overnight soaking**
Cooking time **1 hour 20 minutes**

AFFORDABILITY
2

# FEELING FIT

Being healthy isn't just about eating a well-balanced diet; you also need to take regular exercise. This boosts your endorphins (the happy chemicals in your brain), helps to keep you alert, gets your blood pumping and keeps your immune system on top form.

If you already play a particular sport, it should be easy enough to join a club or find a local team you can train with. But, if you're not a natural gym bunny, it might take a bit of a lifestyle change to incorporate exercise into your daily routine. And there are plenty of opportunities to pull on your tracksuit and work up a sweat without going anywhere near a football pitch, basketball court or a gym.

### WORKOUT DVD OR APP
There are literally hundreds of these on the market, from famous fitness gurus to svelte celebrities, demonstrating their favourite exercises for dropping a few pounds. Involve your housemates and get belly busting in the living room, or keep it quiet and practise your yoga moves in your bedroom.

### COUNT YOUR STEPS
Use an app or buy a cheap pedometer and set yourself the 10k (or 20k if you're feeling ambitious) steps a day challenge. If you walk to college or live on a large campus, it shouldn't be too much extra exertion to reach the target.

### RENT A DOG

Or borrow one, to be more accurate. There are a few websites that link up lonely dogs with people who'd love a dog but can't keep one at home. If you're an animal lover looking for regular exercise, this could be the ideal solution.

### TAKE THE STAIRS

This only works if your college is multi-storey but walking up stairs (or running when you want a real challenge) is a great way to burn calories and build muscle. No special equipment is required and no one will have a clue that you're working out, rather than running late.

### TAKE TO TWO WHEELS

How about getting fit and earning money at the same time? Plenty of food delivery companies employ freelance cyclists and you can work shifts that don't interfere with lectures.

### WEIGH IT UP

Whether it's a set of dumb-bells or a couple of cans of beans, lifting weights is fun and will give you some muscle definition. It's a cheap, easy workout that will give you a well-earned break from writing essays or revising.

# Mushroom
# TOFU SCRAMBLE

1 Heat the oil in a frying pan, add the mushrooms and cook over a high heat, stirring frequently, for 2 minutes until browned and softened.

2 Add the tofu and cook, stirring, for 1 minute.

3 Add the tomatoes to the pan and cook for 2 minutes until starting to soften.

4 Stir in the mushroom ketchup and half the parsley and season with salt and pepper.

5 Serve immediately with hash browns, sprinkled with the remaining parsley.

**VARIATION**

For spinach & sweetcorn tofu scramble, heat 2 tablespoons rapeseed or olive oil in a frying pan. Add 250 g (8 oz) firm tofu, drained, patted dry and crumbled, with 1 teaspoon smoked paprika and cook, stirring, for 2 minutes until hot. Add 75 g (3 oz) frozen or drained canned sweetcorn kernels and heat through for 1 minute, then add 250 g (8 oz) spinach and heat until just wilted. Season with salt and pepper and serve with hash browns or toasted sourdough bread.

2 tablespoons rapeseed or olive oil
200 g (7 oz) chestnut mushrooms, trimmed and quartered
250 g (8 oz) firm tofu, drained, patted dry and crumbled
125 g (4 oz) baby plum tomatoes, halved
1 tablespoon mushroom ketchup
3 tablespoons chopped flat leaf parsley
salt and pepper
hash browns, to serve

Serves **4**
Prep time **15 minutes**
Cooking time **5 minutes**

AFFORDABILITY
1

# Creamy MUSHROOMS WITH WALNUTS

1 tablespoon olive oil
150 g (5 oz) chestnut mushrooms,
   trimmed and sliced
1 garlic clove, crushed
2 sprigs of thyme, plus extra to
   garnish
150 ml (1 pint) soya or oat cream
1 teaspoon soy sauce
50 g (2 oz) chopped walnuts,
   toasted
pepper
bagels, halved and toasted

.................................................

Serves **2**
Prep time **10 minutes**
Cooking time **8 minutes**

.................................................

1 Heat the oil in a frying pan, add the mushrooms and cook over a high heat, stirring frequently, for 2 minutes until browned and softened.

2 Reduce the heat and add the garlic, thyme, soya or oat cream and soy sauce. Simmer, stirring, for 3 minutes, adding a little water if the sauce is too thick.

3 Stir in the walnuts and season with pepper (the soy sauce is salty, so you won't need to season with salt).

4 Spoon the mushroom mixture over the toasted bagels and garnish with thyme sprigs before serving.

# MUSHROOM
## *Risotto cakes*

1 Heat the olive oil in a large, heavy-based frying pan, add the onion, leek, mushrooms and garlic and cook over a medium-high heat for 5–6 minutes until softened and golden.

2 Add the rice and stir well, then add the stock and wine, reduce the heat to a gentle simmer and cook, stirring frequently, until the liquid is almost all absorbed and the rice is tender and cooked through, adding more stock if necessary.

3 Remove from the heat and leave to cool for 20 minutes. The mixture will not only cool but more liquid will be absorbed and the rice will become a little more stodgy.

4 Divide the mixture into 8 and mould each portion into a large patty. Toss liberally in the cornmeal and set aside.

5 Heat the sunflower oil in a frying pan and cook the cakes over a medium-high heat for 2–3 minutes on each side until golden and crisp. Serve hot with a simple dressed salad.

**VARIATION**
For butternut squash risotto cakes, cook the onion and leek over a medium-high heat as above with 200 g (7 oz) peeled, deseeded and finely chopped butternut squash pieces in place of the mushrooms. Reduce the heat, cover and cook for a further 3–4 minutes. Remove the lid, add the rice and continue as above. Serve the cakes with a simple salad.

3 tablespoons olive oil
1 red onion, finely chopped
1 leek, trimmed, cleaned and very thinly sliced
250 g (8 oz) chestnut mushrooms, trimmed and roughly chopped
1 garlic clove, crushed
200 g (7 oz) Arborio rice
600 ml (1 pint) vegetable stock (see page 219), plus extra if needed
150 ml (¼ pint) vegan white wine
75 g (3 oz) cornmeal
4 tablespoons sunflower oil

Serves **4**
Prep time **20 minutes, plus cooling**
Cooking time **25 minutes**

# *Flatbread,* ROASTED VEG & HUMMUS

200 g (7 oz) wholemeal plain
   flour, plus extra for dusting
½ teaspoon salt
1 red pepper, cored, deseeded
   and cut into chunks
1 orange pepper, cored,
   deseeded and cut into chunks
1 green pepper, cored,
   deseeded and cut into chunks
1 large red onion, cut into slim
   wedges
2 tablespoons olive oil
½ teaspoon ground coriander
½ teaspoon cumin seeds

**Hummus**
400 g (14 oz) can chickpeas,
   drained well
finely grated zest and juice of
   1 lemon
3 tablespoons chopped parsley
1 tablespoon tahini
3 tablespoons olive oil
salt and pepper

Serves **4**
Prep time **20 minutes,**
   **plus standing**
Cooking time **20 minutes**

1 Preheat the oven to 220°C (425°F), Gas Mark 7.

2 Mix the flour and salt together in a bowl, then add enough water to bring the mixture together into a dough – about 7-8 tablespoons. Turn out on to a lightly floured surface and knead well until smooth. Return to the bowl, cover with clingfilm and leave in a warm place for 30 minutes.

3 Toss the peppers and onion with the oil in a large roasting tin, then add the coriander and cumin and toss again. Roast for 20 minutes until softened.

4 Meanwhile, blend together all the ingredients for the hummus in a blender or food processor until smooth.

5 Divide the flatbread dough into 4 pieces and roll out each into a 25 cm (10 inch) round.

6 Heat a large frying pan until hot and cook the flatbreads for about 45 seconds on each side until lightly golden, flipping them over with a fish slice.

7 Spread each warm flatbread with some of the hummus, then top with one-quarter of the hot roasted vegetables and fold to serve.

# HEARTY BREAKFAST FRY-UP

1 Cook the potatoes in boiling water for 5 minutes to soften; drain well.

2 Remove as much excess water from the tofu as you can by squeezing it between layers of kitchen paper. Cut into 5 mm (1/4 inch) thick slices and press between further layers of kitchen paper to remove any remaining moisture. Combine the paprika, salt, cumin and mint on a plate. Turn the tofu slices in the mixture to coat.

3 Coarsely grate the potato into a bowl and stir in the oregano and a little salt and pepper. Shape into small cakes by packing the mixture, half at a time, into a small metal cookie cutter, about 8 cm (3 1/2 inches) in diameter. If you don't have one press the mixture into 2 small burger shapes with your hands.

4 Heat 1 tablespoon of the oil in a frying pan. Add the mushrooms and potato cakes and fry gently for about 5 minutes, turning with a fish slice until the mushrooms are tender and the potatoes are golden. Add the tomatoes and fry briefly to soften. Lift out on to serving plates and keep warm.

5 Heat the remaining oil in the pan and fry the tofu for about 2 minutes on each side until golden. Transfer to the plates and sprinkle with parsley and a drizzle of any juices left in the pan.

300 g (10 oz) Charlotte potatoes, scrubbed and cut into small chunks
200 g (7 oz) tofu
1/2 teaspoon smoked paprika
1/2 teaspoon salt
1/4 teaspoon ground cumin
1/4 teaspoon dried mint
1/4 teaspoon dried oregano
3 tablespoons mild olive oil or vegetable oil
2 large portobello mushrooms
2 tomatoes, halved
salt and pepper
chopped parsley, to sprinkle

Serves **2**
Prep time **15 minutes**
Cooking time **15 minutes**

# SOUPS, SALADS, SIDES & SNACKS

CORN, TOMATO & BLACK BEAN SALAD

SEEDED CHIPS WITH RED PEPPER DIP

# ONION, TOMATO &
## CHICKPEA SOUP

2 tablespoons olive oil
2 red onions, roughly chopped
2 garlic cloves, finely chopped
2 teaspoons brown sugar
625 g (1¼ lb) tomatoes, skinned if liked, roughly chopped
2 teaspoons harissa paste
3 teaspoons tomato purée
400 g (14 oz) can chickpeas, drained and rinsed
900 ml (1½ pints) vegetable stock (see page 219)
salt and pepper

Serves **6**
Prep time **15 minutes**
Cooking time **1 hour 10 minutes**

**1** Heat the oil in a large saucepan, add the onions and fry over a low heat for 10 minutes, stirring occasionally, until just beginning to brown around the edges. Stir in the garlic and sugar and cook for 10 more minutes, stirring more frequently as the onions begin to caramelize.

**2** Stir in the tomatoes and harissa paste and fry for 5 minutes. Mix in the tomato purée, chickpeas, stock and salt and pepper and bring to the boil. Cover and simmer for 45 minutes until the tomatoes and onion are very soft. Taste and adjust the seasoning if needed.

**3** Ladle into bowls and serve with warm ciabatta.

**VARIATION**
For chillied red onion & bean soup, make up the soup as above but omit the harissa and add 1 teaspoon of smoked paprika and 1 split dried red chilli when frying the tomatoes, then swap the chickpeas for the same size can of red kidney beans. Serve with warm ciabatta.

AFFORDABILITY 1

# BEETROOT & APPLE *Soup*

1 tablespoon olive oil

1 tablespoon dairy-free spread

2 Bramley apples, peeled, cored and chopped

1 dessert apple, peeled, cored and chopped

625 g (1¼ lb) cooked beetroot, roughly chopped

2 teaspoons caraway seeds

4–5 sprigs of thyme

1.5 litres (2½ pints) vegetable stock (see page 219)

salt and pepper

natural soya yogurt or oat fraîche, to serve

chopped dill, to garnish

Serves **4**

Prep time **10 minutes**

Cooking time **10 minutes**

1 Heat the oil and vegan spread in a pan and fry the apples for 2–3 minutes until golden. Add the cooked beetroot, caraway seeds and thyme and stir-fry for 1–2 minutes.

2 Add the vegetable stock, bring to the boil then cook for 10 minutes.

3 In a blender or with a hand-held blender, whizz the soup until fairly smooth and season to taste.

4 Serve in bowls with soya yogurt or oat fraîche swirled through. Garnish with chopped dill and freshly ground black pepper.

AFFORDABILITY 1

# Chilled GAZPACHO

1. Mix together the vegetables, garlic, chilli and coriander or flat leaf parsley in a large bowl.

2. Add the vinegar, tomato purée, oil and a little salt. Process in batches in a food processor or blender until smooth, scraping the mixture down from the sides of the bowl if necessary.

3. Put the blended mixture into a clean bowl and check the seasoning, adding a little more salt if needed. Chill for up to 24 hours before serving.

4. To serve, ladle the gazpacho into large bowls, scatter with ice cubes and garnish with parsley or coriander, cucumber, pepper and onion.

## VARIATION

For chilled couscous gazpacho, prepare the soup as above, omitting the red peppers, and chill. Place 50 g (2 oz) couscous in a bowl and pour in just enough boiling water to come to 1 cm (½ inch) above the level of the couscous. Cover with clingfilm and set aside for 10 minutes. Uncover, break the couscous up with a fork and allow to cool to room temperature. Stir into the soup just before serving with the chopped herbs and a little harissa on the side. Omit the ice and garnishes.

875 g (1¾ lb) tomatoes, skinned and roughly chopped
½ cucumber, roughly chopped
2 red peppers, cored, deseeded and roughly chopped
1 celery stick, chopped
2 garlic cloves, chopped
½ red chilli, deseeded and sliced
small handful of coriander or flat leaf parsley
2 tablespoons vegan white wine vinegar
2 tablespoons sun-dried tomato paste
4 tablespoons olive oil
salt

### To serve
ice cubes
flat-leaf parsley or coriander, finely chopped
finely diced cucumber, pepper and onion

Serves **6**
Prep time **20 minutes, plus chilling**

AFFORDABILITY 1

# BUTTER BEAN & VEGETABLE *Soup*

1 tablespoon olive oil
2 teaspoons smoked paprika
1 celery stick, sliced
2 carrots, sliced
1 leek, trimmed, cleaned and sliced
600 ml (1 pint) vegetable stock
   (see page 219)
400 g (14 oz) can chopped
   tomatoes
400 g (14 oz) can butter beans,
   drained and rinsed
2 teaspoons chopped rosemary
salt and pepper

Serves **4**
Prep time **10 minutes**
Cooking time **25 minutes**

**1** Heat the oil in a large saucepan, add the paprika, celery, carrots and leek and cook over a medium heat for 3-4 minutes until the vegetables are slightly softened.

**2** Pour over the stock and tomatoes and add the butter beans and rosemary. Season to taste with salt and pepper and bring to the boil, then cover and simmer for 15 minutes, or until the vegetables are just tender.

**3** Ladle into warmed bowls and sprinkle with freshly ground black pepper.

AFFORDABILITY
1

## STUDENT TIP

**STORECUPBOARD STAPLES** Keep your cupboards well stocked with essentials such as pulses, rice, pasta and chopped tomatoes so that when the budget is looking a little sad towards the end of the month, you'll always be able to rustle up a reasonable meal.

# STORECUPBOARD
## SPICY BEAN
# SOUP

1 Heat the vegetable oil in a large, heavy-based saucepan or casserole dish and cook the onion and pepper over a medium-high heat for 4 minutes. Add the garlic and fry for a further 2 minutes until lightly coloured.

2 Stir in the spice mix, then add half the kidney beans and half the black beans, all of the chopped tomatoes, measured water and stock cube. Stir well, bring to the boil and simmer for 10-12 minutes, until slightly thickened.

3 Use a hand-held blender to blend the soup until almost smooth, then stir in the remaining beans and heat through. Ladle into 4 deep bowls and serve immediately with a drizzle of natural soya yogurt and a scattering of tortilla chips.

2 tablespoons vegetable oil
1 large onion, chopped
1 red pepper, cored, deseeded and chopped
2 garlic cloves, chopped
30 g (1¼ oz) sachet Mexican fajita or taco spice mix
400 g (14 oz) can kidney beans, drained and rinsed
400 g (14 oz) can black beans, drained and rinsed
400g (14 oz) can chopped tomatoes
750 ml (1¼ pints) boiling water
1 vegetable stock cube

**To serve**
4 tablespoons natural soya yogurt
25 g (1 oz) tortilla chips (optional)

Serves **4**
Prep time **10 minutes**
Cooking time **20 minutes**

AFFORDABILITY
1

# BUTTERNUT SOUP
## *with peanut pesto*

2 tablespoons olive oil
1 onion, finely chopped
1 butternut squash, about 750 g
(1 lb 10 oz) peeled, deseeded and
cut into chunks
400 g (14 oz) can coconut milk
1 tablespoon vegan Thai green
curry paste
600 ml (1 pint) vegetable stock
(see page 219)

**Pesto**
1 green chilli, deseeded and finely
chopped
2 tablespoons unsalted peanuts,
roughly chopped
4 tablespoons chopped coriander
1 cm (½ inch) piece of fresh root
ginger, peeled and grated
1 tablespoon olive oil
salt and pepper

Serves **6**
Prep time **20 minutes**
Cooking time **40 minutes**

1 Mix all the ingredients for the pesto together in a small serving bowl and season with a little salt and plenty of pepper. Set aside.

2 Heat the oil in a large, heavy-based saucepan, add the onion and butternut squash and cook over a medium-high heat for 5–6 minutes until softened and golden in places.

3 Add the coconut milk, curry paste and stock and bring to the boil, stirring constantly. Cover and simmer gently for 30 minutes until the squash is tender.

4 Transfer the soup in batches to a blender or food processor and blend until smooth. Return to the pan and reheat.

5 Ladle into warmed serving bowls, spoon over a little of the pesto and swirl through.

# BLACK BEAN SOUP
## WITH SOBA NOODLES

1 Cook the noodles in a large saucepan of boiling water for about 5 minutes, or according to the packet instructions, until just tender.

2 Meanwhile, heat the oil in a saucepan over a medium heat, add the spring onions and garlic and stir-fry for 1 minute. Add the chilli, ginger, black bean sauce and stock and bring to the boil.

3 Stir the pak choi or spring greens, soy sauce, sugar and peanuts into the soup, then reduce the heat and simmer gently for 4 minutes.

4 Drain the noodles, rinse with fresh hot water and spoon into 4 warmed bowls. Ladle the soup over the top and serve immediately.

200 g (7 oz) dried soba noodles
2 tablespoons groundnut or
   vegetable oil
1 bunch of spring onions, sliced
2 garlic cloves, roughly chopped
1 red chilli, deseeded and sliced
3.5 cm (1½ inch) piece of fresh
   root ginger, peeled and grated
125 ml (4 fl oz) black bean sauce
   or black bean stir-fry sauce
750 ml (1¼ pints) vegetable stock
   (see page 219)
200 g (7 oz) pak choi or spring
   greens, shredded
2 teaspoons light soy sauce
1 teaspoon caster sugar
50 g (2 oz) raw unsalted peanuts

Serves **4**
Prep time **10 minutes**
Cooking time **8 minutes**

AFFORDABILITY
2

# WINTER CABBAGE
## & GINGER SOUP

1.2 litres (2 pints) vegetable stock (see page 219)
400 g (14 oz) Chinese cabbage, roughly chopped
2 tablespoons finely chopped fresh root ginger
2 star anise
2 tablespoons light soy sauce
½ teaspoon sesame oil
white pepper

Serves **4**
Prep time **10 minutes**
Cooking time **15 minutes**

1 Place the stock in a large saucepan and bring to the boil. Add the cabbage, ginger and star anise to the stock, return to the boil and cook for 10–12 minutes.

2 Remove from the heat and stir in the soy sauce and sesame oil, season with white pepper and ladle into warmed bowls to serve.

### VARIATION

For stir-fried Chinese cabbage with ginger & garlic, remove and discard the outer leaves from ½ Chinese cabbage and cut into large pieces. Crush 3 garlic cloves with a large pinch of salt in a mortar with a pestle until coarsely ground. Heat a wok or large nonstick frying pan over a high heat, add 2 tablespoons of groundnut oil and heat until almost smoking. Add the garlic and 1 tablespoon of peeled and grated fresh root ginger, then immediately add the cabbage and stir-fry, moving the ingredients constantly to prevent the garlic from burning. Cook until the cabbage is heated through but still crunchy. Transfer to a warmed serving plate and season with white pepper before serving.

AFFORDABILITY
1

# CHILLI MISO *Soup*

1 Put the miso paste, soy sauce and stock into a large saucepan and bring to the boil. Reduce the heat, add the noodles and ginger and simmer for 5 minutes.

2 Meanwhile, heat the oil in a wok or large frying pan, add the chilli, sugar snap peas, shallots and baby corn and stir-fry over a medium-high heat for 5 minutes until softened.

3 Transfer the vegetable mixture to the pan with the noodles, add the coriander and stir through. Serve in warmed serving bowls, garnished with the spring onions.

**VARIATION**
For miso soup with ramen peppers & tofu, prepare the miso stock as above, then add 175 g (6 oz) dried ramen noodles in place of the thin rice noodles and simmer for 5 minutes. Heat 1 tablespoon of sesame oil in a wok or large frying pan, add 1 red and 1 yellow pepper, cored, deseeded and thinly sliced, with 75 g (3 oz) roughly chopped sugar snap peas and stir-fry over a medium-high heat for 5 minutes until softened. Add 125 g (4 oz) firm tofu, drained, patted dry and cubed, and gently toss for a few seconds, then transfer the mixture to the pan with the stock and noodles. Stir through, then serve ladled into warmed bowls.

2 tablespoons miso paste
1 tablespoon dark soy sauce
1.4 litres (2½ pints) vegetable stock (see page 219)
150 g (5 oz) dried thin rice noodles
2.5 cm (1 inch) piece of fresh root ginger, peeled and grated
1 tablespoon sesame oil
½ red bird's eye chilli, deseeded and finely chopped
175 g (6 oz) sugar snap peas, diagonally sliced
2 shallots, finely chopped
125 g (4 oz) baby corn, roughly sliced
6 tablespoons chopped coriander
2 spring onions, thinly sliced, to serve

Serves **4**
Prep time **20 minutes**
Cooking time **10 minutes**

AFFORDABILITY 2

# Tapenade
# BRUSCHETTA

1 small ciabatta loaf, cut into 12 slices
3 tablespoons olive oil
1 garlic clove, crushed
1 tablespoon chopped flat leaf parsley
12 marinated sun-dried tomatoes in oil, drained

**Tapenade**
150 g (5 oz) pitted black olives
1 garlic clove
small handful of flat leaf parsley
2 tablespoons capers
1 tablespoon lemon juice
2 tablespoons olive oil
salt and pepper

Makes **12**
Prep time **15 minutes**
Cooking time **10 minutes**

 **1** Arrange the ciabatta slices in a single layer on a baking sheet. Mix the oil, garlic and chopped parsley together and brush over the bread slices.

**2** Bake in a preheated oven, 200°C (400°F), Gas Mark 6, for 10 minutes until golden and crisp.

**3** Meanwhile, put the olives, garlic, parsley, capers, lemon juice and oil in a food processor and process to a coarse paste. Season with salt and pepper.

**4** Spread the tapenade over the ciabatta toast and top each slice with a sun-dried tomato.

**VARIATION**
For artichoke tapenade bruschetta, toast the ciabatta slices as above. Meanwhile, put 75 g (3 oz) each of pitted green olives and drained marinated artichokes in oil (reserving 2 tablespoons of the oil), a small handful of flat leaf parsley, 2 tablespoons of capers, 1 garlic clove, 1 tablespoon of lemon juice and the reserved artichoke oil in a food processor and process to a coarse paste. Season with salt and pepper. Spread the tapenade over the toasts and sprinkle with chopped parsley.

AFFORDABILITY
**1**

# Sweet OAT CAKES

250 g (8 oz) rolled oats
50 g (2 oz) sesame seeds
3 tablespoons poppy seeds
pinch of salt
100 ml (3½ fl oz) boiling water
2 tablespoons agave syrup
7 tablespoons extra virgin olive oil

Makes **20**
Prep time **15 minutes**
Cooking time **15 minutes**

**1** Combine the rolled oats, sesame seeds, poppy seeds and pinch of salt in a large bowl and make a well in the centre.

**2** Pour in the boiling water, agave syrup and olive oil and stir with a wooden spoon to form a soft dough.

**3** Shape the dough into 20 balls the size of a walnut. Place them on a nonstick baking sheet and flatten them with the palm of your hand to make 8 cm (3½ inch) rounds.

**4** Bake in a preheated oven, 180°C (350°F), Gas Mark 4, for about 15 minutes until golden.

**5** Remove the oat cakes from the oven and transfer to a wire rack to cool. Serve with vegan hard cheese and grapes.

AFFORDABILITY **1**

## STUDENT TIP

**DON'T FORGET YOUR BAGS** Always take a plastic or reusable shopping bag with you when leave the house so you'll never be charged at the shop (and you won't be adding to landfill). And when ordering online, request delivery without bags.

# SMOKY
## TOFU NUGGETS
### *on toast*

1. Preheat the oven to 180°C (350°F), Gas Mark 4. Combine the soy sauce and avocado oil in a small bowl, then add the smoked tofu and mix well.

2. Spoon the tofu mixture on to an oiled baking sheet and place in the oven for 10-15 minutes or until crispy.

3. Heat the soya milk to just below boiling point. Add the rapeseed oil and mix thoroughly with a hand-held whisk. Add the vinegar, whisking all the time. Add the potato flour, mustard, tomato sauce and bouillon powder to the milk mixture, whisk again and bring back to the boil, stirring constantly.

4. Spread the slices of bread with the yeast extract. Mix the baked tofu with the milk mixture, then spread on the bread.

5. Place the bread on the baking sheet and bake in the oven for 10 minutes until golden and starting to bubble. Cut each slice into wedges, sprinkle with black pepper and serve.

2 teaspoons soy sauce
2 teaspoons avocado oil or olive oil
50 g (2 oz) smoked tofu or vegan bacon or ham, finely chopped
125 ml (4 fl oz) sweetened soya milk
125 ml (4 fl oz) rapeseed oil
2 teaspoons cider vinegar
1 tablespoon potato flour
1 teaspoon English mustard
1 tablespoon vegan tomato sauce
1 teaspoon vegan bouillon powder
4 slices of wholemeal bread
1 teaspoon yeast extract
black pepper

Serves **2**
Prep time **10 minutes**
Cooking time **20-25 minutes**

AFFORDABILITY
2

# Egg-free OMELETTE

1 Heat 1 tablespoon of olive oil in a large nonstick frying pan with a lid, then gently fry the onion, mushrooms, peppers and tofu over a medium heat for about 5 minutes, stirring occasionally.

2 Put the flour, baking powder, bouillon powder, milk, vinegar, mustard, soy sauce, herbes de Provence, 2 tablespoons of the remaining olive oil and salt and pepper in a large jug and whisk with a fork.

3 Fold in the soyannaise, then pour the mixture on to the vegetables in the frying pan. Cook gently for 3-4 minutes with the pan covered so that the steam partly cooks the top.

4 Slide the omelette on to a plate, then oil the pan, place it upside down over the plate and flip it over. Return the pan to the heat and brown the other side of the omelette. Serve hot with a mixed salad.

4 tablespoons olive oil
1 onion, chopped
6 mushrooms, sliced
½ red pepper, cored, deseeded and chopped
½ green pepper, cored, deseeded and chopped
50 g (2 oz) tofu, crumbled
3 heaped tablespoons strong white flour
½ teaspoon baking powder
2 heaped teaspoons vegan bouillon powder
5 tablespoons soya milk
1 tablespoon cider vinegar
1 teaspoon mustard
1 tablespoon soy sauce
2 teaspoons herbes de Provence
1 tablespoon Soyannaise (see page 218)
salt and pepper

Serves **2**
Prep time **10 minutes**
Cooking time **10 minutes**

AFFORDABILITY
1

# ORANGE & AVOCADO *Salad*

4 large juicy oranges
2 small ripe avocados
2 teaspoons cardamom pods
3 tablespoons olive oil
1 tablespoon agave syrup
pinch of allspice
2 teaspoons lemon juice
salt and pepper
sprigs of watercress, to garnish

Serves **4**
Prep time **20 minutes**

1 Cut the skin and the white membrane off the oranges. Working over a bowl to catch the juice, cut between the membranes to remove the segments.

2 Peel and stone the avocados, slice the flesh and toss gently with the orange segments. Pile on to serving plates.

3 Reserve a few whole cardamom pods for garnishing. Crush the remainder using a pestle and mortar to extract the seeds or place them in a small bowl and crush with the end of a rolling pin. Pick out and discard the pods.

4 Mix the seeds with the oil, agave syrup, allspice and lemon juice. Season to taste with salt and pepper and stir in the reserved orange juice.

5 Garnish the salad with sprigs of watercress and the reserved cardamom pods and serve with the dressing spooned over the top.

AFFORDABILITY

1

# BROCCOLI, PEA & AVOCADO SALAD

1 Toast the sesame and chia seeds in a dry pan over a medium heat, shaking the pan a couple of times, for 30 seconds until golden. Tip the seeds out of the pan and leave to cool.

2 Blanch the broccoli with the peas in a large saucepan of boiling water for 2 minutes until the broccoli is just tender but still firm. Drain, rinse under cold water and drain again.

3 Tip the broccoli and peas into a large salad bowl. Add the avocado, spinach leaves, alfalfa, if using, mint and toasted seeds.

4 Whisk the lime juice, sesame oil and ginger together in a jug and season with salt and pepper. Pour over the salad and toss well to mix.

## VARIATION
For spinach, beetroot & pomegranate salad, toast the sesame and chia seeds as above. Put 125 g (4 oz) baby spinach leaves in a salad bowl with 175 g (6 oz) chopped Sweetfire beetroot (cooked beetroot infused with a sweet chilli marinade), 2 sliced celery sticks, 1 large ripe avocado, peeled, stoned and chopped, 25 g (1 oz) sprouting alfalfa, a small handful of chopped flat leaf parsley leaves and the toasted seeds. Make the lime juice dressing as above, then pour over the salad and toss well to mix.

---

1 tablespoon sesame seeds
1 tablespoon chia seeds
350 g (12 oz) broccoli, cut into
  small florets
150 g (5 oz) frozen peas
1 large ripe avocado, peeled,
  stoned and chopped
125 g (4 oz) baby spinach leaves
25 g (1 oz) sprouting alfalfa
  (optional)
2 tablespoons chopped mint
juice of 1 lime
2 teaspoons sesame oil
1.5 cm (¾ inch) piece of fresh
  root ginger, peeled and grated
salt and pepper

---

Serves **4**
Prep time **20 minutes,**
  **plus cooling**
Cooking time **5 minutes**

AFFORDABILITY
1

# CARROT & CASHEW NUT Salad

75 g (3 oz) unsalted cashew nuts
2 tablespoons black mustard
 seeds
500 g (1 lb 2 oz) carrots, peeled
 and coarsely grated
1 red pepper, cored, deseeded and
 thinly sliced
3 tablespoons chopped chervil or
 flat leaf parsley
2 spring onions, thinly sliced

**Dressing**
2 tablespoons avocado oil
2 tablespoons raspberry vinegar
1 tablespoon wholegrain mustard
pinch of sugar
salt and pepper

Serves **4**
Prep time **10 minutes**
Cooking time **6-10 minutes**

**1** Heat a dry nonstick frying pan over a medium-low heat and toast the cashew nuts, stirring frequently, for 5-8 minutes, or until golden brown. Tip them on to a small plate and leave to cool. Add the mustard seeds to the pan and toast them for 1-2 minutes, or until they start to pop.

**2** Mix together the mustard seeds, carrots, red pepper, chervil or parsley and spring onions in a large bowl.

**3** Whisk together all the dressing ingredients in a small bowl, then pour on to the grated carrot salad. Mix the salad thoroughly to coat and heap it into serving bowls.

**4** Chop the cashew nuts coarsely and scatter over the salad. Serve immediately.

# COCONUT, CARROT & SPINACH SALAD

1. Place the spinach in a large bowl with the carrot and coconut, and toss together lightly.

2. Heat the oil a small frying pan over a medium heat. Add the mustard and cumin seeds and stir-fry for 20-30 seconds until fragrant and the mustard seeds start to pop.

3. Remove from the heat, and scatter over the salad. Pour over the lime and orange juice. Season well and toss before serving.

300 g (10 oz) baby spinach, finely chopped
1 carrot, peeled and coarsely grated
25 g (1 oz) fresh coconut, grated
2 tablespoons groundnut oil
2 teaspoons black mustard seeds
1 teaspoon cumin seeds
juice of 1 lime
juice of 1 orange
salt and pepper

Serves **4**
Prep time **10 minutes**
Cooking time **1 minute**

## STUDENT TIP

**DITCH THE BUS** This obviously depends on how far away from campus you live but it's easy to get your daily exercise quota by simply walking or cycling rather than relying on public transport. And you'll save money, too.

AFFORDABILITY
1

# CHICKPEA & CHILLI SALAD

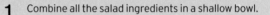

2 × 400g (14 oz) cans chickpeas,
  drained and rinsed
2 plum tomatoes, roughly chopped
4 spring onions, thinly sliced
1 red chilli, deseeded and thinly
  sliced
4 tablespoons roughly chopped
  coriander leaves

**Lemon dressing**
2 tablespoons lemon juice
1 garlic clove, crushed
2 tablespoons olive oil
salt and pepper

**To serve**
grilled pitta bread, cut into thin
  fingers

Serves **4**
Prep time **10 minutes, plus
  10 minutes standing**

**1** Combine all the salad ingredients in a shallow bowl.

**2** Put all the dressing ingredients in a screw-top jar, season to taste with salt and pepper and shake well. Pour over the salad and toss well to coat all the ingredients.

**3** Cover the salad and leave to stand at room temperature for about 10 minutes to allow the flavours to mingle. Serve with the grilled pitta bread fingers.

**VARIATION**
For white bean & sun-dried tomato salad, combine 2 x 400 g (14 oz) cans cannellini beans, drained and rinsed, 125 g (4 oz) sun-dried tomatoes in oil, drained and roughly chopped, 1 tablespoon of chopped and pitted black olives, 2 teaspoons of drained and rinsed capers, and 2 teaspoons of chopped thyme leaves. Toss in the lemon dressing and let stand as above, then serve with toasted slices of ciabatta bread.

# CORN, TOMATO &
# BLACK BEAN SALAD

4 corn cobs, leaves and fibres
  removed
250 g (8 oz) cherry tomatoes,
  halved
400 g (14 oz) can black beans,
  drained and rinsed
1 red onion, finely diced
1 avocado, peeled, stoned and
  diced
small bunch of coriander, roughly
  chopped

**Dressing**
juice of 1 lime
2 tablespoons rapeseed oil
2–3 drops Tabasco sauce

Serves **4**
Prep time **10 minutes**
Cooking time **10 minutes**

1 Cook the corn cobs in boiling water for 7–10 minutes. Cool briefly under running cold water then slice off the kernels with a knife.

2 Put the kernels in a large bowl with the tomatoes, black beans, onion and avocado and mix with the coriander.

3 Make the dressing by mixing together the lime juice, oil and Tabasco. Drizzle the dressing over the salad, stir carefully to combine and serve immediately.

# PACK YOUR LUNCH

A student budget can slip through your fingers – bus fares, books, coffees, evenings out with friends; it all adds up. So, if there's any way to make savings, it can make a big difference at the end of the month when your bank account is bare. Making your own lunch to take to university is quick and easy, and could save you a small fortune over a term or two. It will take a bit of forward planning and maybe an earlier start, but it's worth it. The other bonus is you get to choose your lunch, rather than being stuck with the solitary vegan-friendly selection at the counter.

**COUSCOUS SALAD BOWL**
Mix steamed and cooled couscous with chopped sun-dried tomatoes, olives and chickpeas and pack in a plastic storage box.

**VEGETABLE WRAP**
Fill a wrap with baby spinach, grated carrot, grated beetroot and cucumber batons. Add a dollop of dairy-free pesto, vegan mayonnaise or Soyannaise (see page 218), roll it up and wrap in kitchen foil to keep fresh.

## PASTA SALAD

The options are almost infinite when it comes to pasta. You can cook and cool sufficient pasta for two or three servings. Keep in an airtight container in the fridge and prepare a different lunch each day. Cherry tomatoes, basil, dairy-free pesto, pine nuts, steamed and cooled broccoli and petit pois are all easy additions.

## GUACAMOLE

Mash an avocado with a little lime juice and a pinch of chilli flakes for a delicious homemade dip. Pack in a small plastic storage box and take a heap of fresh breadsticks to scoop it up.

## SOUP

Treat yourself to a flask and you can enjoy hot soup during the winter. Make a big batch and it will keep in the fridge for two or three days. Chunky vegetable soups are filling and healthy, and by adding tiny pasta shapes such as orzo you can turn it into even more of a meal.

## SANDWICH

There's nothing wrong with a simple sandwich for lunch and making your own is much cheaper than buying them. Leaves, avocado slices, grated or sliced vegetables, plum tomatoes, vegan cheese and a slather of chutney or pickle will liven up your lunchtime.

# BULGAR SALAD WITH ROASTED PEPPERS *on little gem*

AFFORDABILITY **1**

1 Tip the bulgar wheat into a bowl, pour over the measured boiling water, stir, then cover and leave for 10–15 minutes until the grains are tender.

2 Add the tomato purée, lemon juice, olive oil, chilli and some salt to the bulgar wheat mixture and mix thoroughly.

3 Add the roasted red peppers, spring onions and tomatoes, together with the parsley and mint, and mix well.

4 Arrange the lettuce leaves around the edges of a platter with the bulgar salad in the centre. Use the leaves to scoop up the bulgar mixture and eat.

200 g (7 oz) fine-ground bulgar wheat
125 ml (4 fl oz) boiling water
1 tablespoon tomato purée
juice of 1½ lemons
5 tablespoons extra virgin olive oil
1 red chilli, finely chopped
200 g (7 oz) roasted red peppers (from a jar), drained and diced
8 spring onions, thinly sliced
300 g (10 oz) tomatoes, diced
50 g (2 oz) flat leaf parsley, roughly chopped
25 g (1 oz) mint leaves, roughly chopped
4 little gem lettuces, leaves separated
salt

Serves **4**
Prep time **30 minutes**

# QUINOA, COURGETTE & POMEGRANATE SALAD

1 Cook the quinoa following the packet instructions, then drain and rinse under cold water. Drain again.

2 Cut the ends off the courgette then cut into ribbons using a potato peeler.

3 Whisk together the vinegar and 2 tablespoons of the oil in a jug and season with salt and pepper.

4 Put the quinoa, courgette ribbons and remaining ingredients in a large bowl, pour over the dressing and toss everything together and serve.

75 g (3 oz) quinoa
1 large courgette
1 tablespoon vegan white wine vinegar
4 tablespoons olive oil
4 spring onions, thinly sliced
100 g (3½ oz) cherry tomatoes, halved
1 red chilli, finely chopped
100 g (3½ oz) pomegranate seeds (or seeds of ½ pomegranate)
small handful of finely chopped flat leaf parsley
salt and pepper

Serves **4**
Prep time **20 minutes**

AFFORDABILITY 1

# GINGERED TOFU
# & MANGO SALAD

25 g (1 oz) fresh root ginger, peeled and grated
2 tablespoons light soy sauce
1 garlic clove, finely chopped
1 tablespoon seasoned rice vinegar
125 g (4 oz) firm silken tofu, cut into 1 cm (½ inch) cubes
2 tablespoons groundnut or vegetable oil
1 bunch of spring onions, sliced diagonally into 1.5 cm (¾ inch) lengths
40 g (1½ oz) cashew nuts
1 small mango, peeled, stoned and sliced
½ small iceberg lettuce, shredded
2 tablespoons water

Serves **2**
Prep time **15 minutes,
   plus marinating**
Cooking time **5 minutes**

**1** Mix together the ginger, soy sauce, garlic and vinegar in a small bowl. Add the tofu to the bowl and toss the ingredients together. Leave to marinate for 15 minutes.

**2** Lift the tofu from the marinade with a fork, drain and reserve the marinade for later.

**3** Heat the oil in a frying pan over a medium heat, add the tofu pieces and gently fry for 3 minutes, or until golden. Remove with a slotted spoon and keep warm. Add the spring onions and cashew nuts to the pan and fry quickly for 30 seconds. Add the mango slices to the pan and cook for 30 seconds, or until heated through.

**4** Pile the lettuce on to serving plates and scatter the tofu, spring onions, mango and cashew nuts over the top. Heat the marinade juices in the pan with the measured water, pour the mixture over the salad and serve immediately.

**VARIATION**
For tofu & sugar snap salad, marinate and fry the tofu as above, reserving the marinade. Add the spring onions and cashew nuts to the pan, also adding 1 red chilli, thinly sliced, and 100 g (3½ oz) halved sugar snap peas. Omit the mango. Fry for 1 minute until heated through, then gently toss in the fried tofu. Add the juice of ½ lime and 2 tablespoons of water to the reserved marinade and drizzle it over the salad before serving on the lettuce.

# SOY TOFU SALAD
## WITH CORIANDER

500 g (1 lb 2 oz) firm tofu, drained
and cut into bite-sized pieces
6 spring onions, finely shredded
10 tablespoons roughly chopped
coriander leaves
1 large mild red chilli, deseeded
and thinly sliced
4 tablespoons light soy sauce
2 teaspoons sesame oil

Serves **4**
Prep time **10 minutes,**
**plus standing**

1 Carefully arrange the tofu on a serving plate in a single layer.
Sprinkle over the spring onions, coriander and chilli.

2 Drizzle over the soy sauce and oil, then leave to stand at room
temperature for 10 minutes before serving.

### STUDENT TIP

**USE YOUR SMARTPHONE** From step counters
to shopping calculators and recipe planners, your
smartphone is so much more than a social media
hub. Use it to plan ahead, save money when you're
shopping and to maintain a healthier lifestyle.

AFFORDABILITY

# *Fatoush* SALAD

1 First make the dressing. Whisk the olive oil, lemon juice, garlic and sumac together in a bowl. Season to taste.

2 To make the salad, combine the pitta pieces, tomatoes, cucumber, radishes, red onion, lettuce leaves and mint leaves in a large bowl.

3 When ready to serve, pour the dressing over the salad and gently mix together to coat the salad evenly.

**VARIATION**
For a Middle Eastern couscous salad, replace the pitta bread with 400 g (14 oz) cooked couscous. Pour over the dressing, toss to mix well, and serve.

1 pitta bread, torn into small pieces
6 plum tomatoes, deseeded and roughly chopped
½ cucumber, peeled and roughly chopped
10 radishes, sliced
1 red onion, roughly chopped
1 small little gem lettuce, leaves separated
small handful of fresh mint leaves

**Dressing**
200 ml (7 fl oz) olive oil
juice of 3 lemons
1 garlic clove, crushed
2 teaspoons sumac (or ½ teaspoon ground cumin)
salt and pepper

Serves **4**
Prep time **20 minutes**

AFFORDABILITY 1

# MEDITERRANEAN
## Potato salad

450 g (1 lb) potatoes, peeled and
  cut into chunks
pinch of saffron threads
125 g (4 oz) sunblush tomatoes,
  halved
75 g (3 oz) pitted black olives,
  roughly chopped
6 tablespoons olive oil
4 tablespoons chia seeds
5 tablespoons chopped basil
  leaves
3 tablespoons capers
salt and pepper

Serves **4**
Prep time **10 minutes,
  plus cooling**
Cooking time **20 minutes**

1  Pour over just enough cold water to cover the potatoes in a
   saucepan and add the saffron. Bring to the boil, then cover
   and simmer very gently for 15 minutes until tender and
   cooked through. Drain and leave to cool.

2  Put the tomatoes, olives, oil, chia seeds, basil and capers into
   a large bowl, add the cooled potatoes and gently toss
   together. Season with a little salt and plenty of pepper.

3  Divide the salad between 4 serving bowls and serve with
   fresh crusty bread or a simple rocket salad, if liked.

### VARIATION
For Mediterranean pasta salad, cook 225 g (7½ oz) dried pasta in
a large saucepan of lightly salted boiling water for 8-10 minutes
until just tender. Drain well, rinse under cold water and drain again.
Put 125 g (4 oz) roughly chopped sunblush tomatoes, 75 g (3 oz)
roughly chopped pitted black olives, 6 tablespoons of olive oil,
4 tablespoons of chia seeds, 5 tablespoons of chopped basil
leaves and 3 tablespoons of capers in a large bowl. Combine with
the pasta and toss well so that all the ingredients are well mixed.
Season with salt and pepper before serving.

# HERB-ROASTED
## NEW POTATOES

1 Put the oil into a roasting tin and place in a preheated oven, 200°C (400°F), Gas Mark 6, for 5 minutes until hot.

2 Add the potatoes, garlic and herb sprigs, season well with salt and pepper and turn to coat in the oil.

3 Return to the oven and roast for 40–45 minutes, turning occasionally, until the potatoes are crisp and tender. Serve hot.

**VARIATION**

For crushed new potatoes with spring onions & mustard, cook 1 kg (2 lb) scrubbed new potatoes in a large saucepan of lightly salted boiling water for 15 minutes, or until tender. Drain well, return to the pan and add 2 tablespoons of olive oil and 1 tablespoon wholegrain mustard. Crush with a fork until the potatoes are broken up but not mashed, then stir in 4 chopped spring onions. Season to taste with salt and pepper and serve immediately.

2 tablespoons olive oil
1 kg (2 lb) new potatoes, scrubbed
4 garlic cloves, peeled but left whole
2 sprigs of rosemary
2 sprigs of thyme
1 sprig of sage
salt and pepper

Serves **6**
Prep time **10 minutes**
Cooking time **45-50 minutes**

AFFORDABILITY

# NEW POTATO, BASIL & PINE NUT
# SALAD

1 kg (2 lb) new potatoes, scrubbed
4 tablespoons extra virgin olive oil
1½ tablespoons vegan white wine
   vinegar
50 g (2 oz) pine nuts
½ bunch of basil, leaves picked
salt and pepper

Serves **4-6**
Prep time **10 minutes,**
   **plus cooling**
Cooking time **15-18 minutes**

**1** Cook the potatoes in a large saucepan of lightly salted boiling water for 12-15 minutes until tender. Drain well and transfer to a large bowl. Cut any large potatoes in half.

**2** Whisk together the oil, vinegar and a little salt and pepper in a jug. Add half to the potatoes, stir well and leave to cool completely.

**3** Toast the pine nuts in a dry frying pan over a medium heat, shaking the pan occasionally, for 2-3 minutes until golden. Tip out of the pan and leave to cool.

**4** Mix the toasted pine nuts, remaining dressing and basil with the potatoes, toss well and then serve.

# SPICED POTATO CURRY

1 Heat the oil in a large nonstick wok or frying pan over a medium-high heat. Add the mustard seeds, chilli powder, cumin seeds and curry leaves. Stir-fry for 1-2 minutes until fragrant.

2 Add the ground spices and potatoes. Season to taste and stir-fry briskly over a high heat for 4-5 minutes. Remove from the heat and stir in the coriander. Squeeze over the lemon juice just before serving.

## VARIATION

For quick curried spinach & potato sauté, follow the recipe above, then after the potatoes have been stir-fried for 4-5 minutes, gently fold in 100 g (3½ oz) baby spinach. Stir-fry for 1-2 minutes, then remove from the heat, squeeze over 4 tablespoons of lemon juice and serve immediately with steamed rice or bread.

1 tablespoon groundnut oil
1-2 teaspoons black mustard seeds
1 teaspoon chilli powder or paprika
4 teaspoons cumin seeds
8-10 curry leaves
2 teaspoons ground cumin
2 teaspoons ground coriander
1 teaspoon ground turmeric
500 g (1 lb 2 oz) potatoes, peeled, boiled and cut into 2.5 cm (1 inch) cubes
6 tablespoons chopped coriander leaves
4 tablespoons lemon juice
salt and pepper

Serves **4**
Prep time **20 minutes**
Cooking time **6-8 minutes**

AFFORDABILITY
1

# ROAST
# VEGETABLES

1 small butternut squash
2 beetroots
1 potato
½ cassava
2 carrots
2 red onions
1 courgette
125 ml (4 fl oz) avocado oil
1 tablespoon soy sauce
4 whole garlic cloves
2 teaspoons rosemary leaves
2 teaspoons chopped fennel
  fronds
salt and pepper

Serves **8**
Prep time **20 minutes**
Cooking time **45-50 minutes**

**1** Preheat the oven to 180°C (350°F), Gas Mark 4. Trim all the vegetables, then cut them into finger-sized pieces.

**2** Place the avocado oil and soy sauce into a large bowl and mix well. Dip all the vegetable pieces and garlic cloves in so that they are well coated.

**3** Arrange the squash, beetroot, potato and cassava on a baking tray and bake for 20 minutes.

**4** Turn these vegetables over, then add the carrot, onions, courgette and garlic. Sprinkle with the rosemary and fennel, season with salt and pepper, then return the tray to the oven for a further 25-30 minutes.

**5** Serve with a variety of dips, such as hummus, Soyannaise (see page 218) or sweet chilli sauce, and some warmed bread.

# SUMMER VEGETABLE
# TEMPURA

1 Mix the dipping sauce ingredients together in a serving bowl and set aside.

2 Half-fill a deep saucepan with vegetable oil and heat to 180–190°C (350–375°F), or until a cube of bread dropped into the oil browns in 30 seconds. Just before the oil is hot enough, using a hand whisk, quickly beat the flour, cornflour, salt and sparkling water together in a bowl to make a slightly lumpy batter.

3 Dip one-third of the vegetables into the batter until coated and then drop straight into the hot oil. Fry for 2 minutes until crisp. Remove from the pan with a slotted spoon, drain on kitchen paper and keep warm in a low oven.

4 Fry the remaining vegetables in 2 more batches. Serve hot with the dipping sauce.

vegetable oil, for deep-frying
75 g (3 oz) plain flour
2 tablespoons cornflour
pinch of salt
200 ml (7 fl oz) ice-cold sparkling water
1 red pepper, cored, deseeded and cut into strips
150 g (5 oz) thin asparagus spears, trimmed
1 courgette, trimmed and sliced

**Dipping sauce**
2 tablespoons sweet chilli sauce
2 tablespoons soy sauce
1 teaspoon finely grated lemon zest
1 tablespoon lemon juice

Serves **4**
Prep time **20 minutes**
Cooking time **15 minutes**

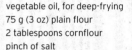

AFFORDABILITY
1

# ITALIAN VEGETABLE
## *Kebabs*

1 Place the chopped vegetables in a large bowl and toss in the olive oil, lemon juice, basil and salt and pepper.

2 Thread the vegetables on to metal skewers and grill or barbecue over a medium heat for 10-12 minutes, turning occasionally, until cooked. Serve immediately.

2 red peppers, cored, deseeded and chopped
1 yellow pepper, cored, deseeded and chopped
2 courgettes, cut into thick slices
1 large red onion, cut into wedges
2 tablespoons olive oil
2 tablespoons lemon juice
2 tablespoons torn basil leaves
salt and pepper

Makes **4**
Prep time **10 minutes**
Cooking time **12 minutes**

### STUDENT TIP

**SHOP SEASONAL** It's healthier and often cheaper to buy fruit and vegetables that are in season and you also cut down on food miles. With farmers' markets becoming increasingly popular, you should find it easy to buy locally farmed produce on your doorstop.

AFFORDABILITY
1

# AUBERGINE
## WITH CAPER & MINT PESTO

1 Put the aubergine slices in a large bowl, pour over the oil and toss well, using both hands to coat as evenly as possible. The oil will be absorbed fast, so work as quickly as possible. Set aside for 10 minutes while you make the pesto.

2 Mix all the pesto ingredients together in a jug. Season with a little salt and pepper.

3 Heat a griddle pan until smoking, then lay several of the aubergine slices on to the hot pan in a single layer and cook over a high heat for 1-2 minutes on each side until lightly charred and soft.

4 Transfer the aubergine to a heatproof platter and keep warm in a low oven while cooking the remaining slices.

5 Drizzle or spoon some of the pesto over the aubergine slices and serve with warm pitta bread, with the remaining pesto on the side.

2 aubergines, trimmed and sliced
150 ml (¼ pint) extra virgin olive oil
warm pitta bread, to serve

**Pesto**
finely grated zest and juice of 1 lemon
3 tablespoons olive oil
2 tablespoons vegan red wine vinegar
4 tablespoons chopped mint leaves, plus extra leaves to garnish
2 tablespoons capers, roughly chopped
1 garlic clove, roughly chopped
1 teaspoon sugar
salt and pepper

Serves **4**
Prep time **20 minutes**
Cooking time **15 minutes**

AFFORDABILITY
1

# BROCCOLI
## WITH GARLIC & CHILLI

400 g (13 oz) broccoli florets
2 tablespoons groundnut oil
2 garlic cloves, thinly sliced
2 teaspoons peeled and grated
  fresh root ginger
1-2 teaspoons dried chilli flakes
salt and pepper

Serves **4**
Prep time **10 minutes**
Cooking time **5 minutes**

1 Cut the broccoli florets lengthways into thin slices.

2 Bring a large saucepan of lightly salted water to the boil. Add the broccoli and blanch for 1-2 minutes. Drain and set aside.

3 Heat the oil in a large nonstick wok or frying pan over a high heat. Swirl the oil around, add the garlic, ginger and chilli flakes and sizzle for 20-30 seconds until fragrant.

4 Add the broccoli to the pan and stir-fry for about 1-2 minutes until just tender. Season with salt and pepper and serve immediately with cooked rice or noodles.

**VARIATION**
For cauliflower with garlic, chilli & sesame, follow the recipe above, replacing the broccoli with 400 g (13 oz) cauliflower florets. When the dish is ready, sprinkle over 2 tablespoons of toasted sesame seeds and serve immediately.

AFFORDABILITY **1**

# Pak choi
## WITH CHILLI & GINGER

1 tablespoon groundnut oil
½ chilli, sliced into rings
1 tablespoon peeled and chopped
  fresh root ginger
large pinch of salt
500 g (1 lb 2 oz) pak choi, leaves
  separated
100 ml (3½ fl oz) water
¼ teaspoon sesame oil

. . . . . . . . . . . . . . . . . . . . . . . . . . . . . . .
Serves **4**
Prep time **5 minutes**
Cooking time **5 minutes**
. . . . . . . . . . . . . . . . . . . . . . . . . . . . . . .

1 Heat the groundnut oil in a wok or large frying pan over
a high heat until the oil starts to shimmer. Add the chilli,
ginger and salt and stir-fry for 15 seconds.

2 Tip the pak choi into the pan and stir-fry for 1 minute, then
add the measured water and continue cooking and stirring
until the pak choi is tender and the water has evaporated.

3 Add the sesame oil to the pan, toss well and serve
immediately.

# Spicy BEETROOT & WALNUT PARCELS

300 g (10 oz) cooked beetroot
3 tablespoons olive oil
1 small red onion, chopped
2 celery sticks, chopped
2 teaspoons cumin seeds
75 g (3 oz) broken walnuts
150 g (5 oz) vegan mayonnaise
   or Soyannaise (see page 218)
2 teaspoons harissa or chipotle
   paste
4 sheets of filo pastry
salt and pepper
salad leaves, to serve

Serves **3-4**
Prep time **25 minutes**
Cooking time **30 minutes**

1 Preheat the oven to 200°C (400°F), Gas Mark 6. Coarsely grate the beetroot into a bowl.

2 Heat 1 tablespoon of the oil in a frying pan and fry the onion and celery for 3 minutes to soften. Add to the beetroot, along with the cumin seeds, walnuts and a little salt and pepper. Mix well.

3 Beat together the mayonnaise and harissa or chipotle paste and transfer to a small serving dish.

4 Lay one sheet of filo pastry on the work surface and brush with a little of the remaining oil. Lay a second sheet of pastry on top. Cut into six squares.

5 Spoon a little of the beetroot mixture on to the centre of each square so you use about half the filling altogether, spreading the mixture towards the edges. Fold 2 opposite sides of one square over the filling, then roll up from an unfolded edge to make a parcel. Place on a baking sheet. Repeat with the remaining 5 squares, then use the remaining filo sheets and filling to make 6 more parcels. Brush with the remaining oil.

6 Bake for 20-25 minutes until crisp and golden. Serve with the spicy mayonnaise and salad leaves.

# SPINACH DAHL
## *with*
## CHERRY TOMATOES

1 Place the lentils in a sieve and rinse under cold running water until the water runs clear. Drain and transfer to a wide saucepan with the coconut milk, stock, cumin, coriander, turmeric and ginger.

2 Bring the mixture to the boil, skimming off any scum as it rises to the surface, and then cover. Reduce the heat and simmer for 15-20 minutes, stirring occasionally to prevent the mixture from sticking to the base of the saucepan. Stir in the spinach and cherry tomatoes and cook for 6-8 minutes, or until the lentils are soft and tender, adding a little stock or water if the mixture seems too thick.

3 Meanwhile make the tarka. Heat the oil in a small frying pan and sauté the shallots, garlic, ginger, chilli powder and cumin and mustard seeds, stirring often. Cook for 3-4 minutes until the shallots are lightly browned, and then combine this mixture into the cooked lentils.

4 Stir in the garam masala and chopped coriander, then check the seasoning. Serve with naan bread or rice.

300 g (10 oz) red split lentils
200 ml (7 fl oz) coconut milk
600 ml (1 pint) vegetable stock (see page 219)
1 teaspoon ground cumin
1 teaspoon ground coriander
1 teaspoon ground turmeric
1 teaspoon ground ginger
300 g (10 oz) spinach, chopped
200 g (7 oz) cherry tomatoes
¼ teaspoon garam masala
25 g (1 oz) coriander (leaves and stalks), finely chopped
salt and pepper

**Tarka**
2 tablespoons sunflower oil
4 shallots, thinly sliced
3 garlic cloves, thinly sliced
1 teaspoon finely chopped fresh root ginger
¼ teaspoon chilli powder
2 teaspoons cumin seeds
1 teaspoon black mustard seeds

Serves **4**
Prep time **5 minutes**
Cooking time **30 minutes**

AFFORDABILITY
1

# COURGETTE & AUBERGINE
# FAJITAS

750 g (1½ lb) courgettes, cut into chip-sized pieces
2 medium aubergines, about 500g (1 lb 2 oz), cut into chip-sized pieces
2 red onions, sliced
4 tablespoons mild olive oil or vegetable oil
2 teaspoons ground cumin
2 ripe avocados
1 garlic clove, crushed
1 teaspoon lime juice
160 ml (5½ fl oz) can coconut cream, chilled
200 g (7 oz) cherry tomatoes, chopped
2 spring onions, finely chopped
1 red chilli, deseeded and finely chopped
3 tablespoons chopped coriander
8 plain, wholemeal or seeded wraps
100 g (3½ oz) Cheddar-style vegan cheese, finely grated
salt and pepper

Makes **8**
Prep time **40 minutes**
Cooking time **1¼ - 1½ hours**

1 Preheat the oven to 200°C (400°F), Gas Mark 6. Put the courgettes, aubergines and onions in a roasting tin. Drizzle with the oil and sprinkle with the cumin and a little salt and pepper. Toss the ingredients together and bake for 1¼ -1½ hours, turning the vegetables several times during cooking.

2 Mash the avocado in a bowl and beat in the garlic, lime juice and plenty of freshly ground black pepper. In a separate bowl whip the coconut cream using a hand-held electric whisk or balloon whisk until softly peaking.

3 Combine the tomatoes with the spring onions, chilli and coriander and put to one side. Seal the wraps in a sheet of foil and place on an oven shelf below the roasting vegetables. Heat through for 10 minutes.

4 To serve, spoon the vegetables down the centres of the wraps, top with the tomato salsa, coconut cream, avocado mash and Cheddar-style vegan cheese. Wrap and serve.

AFFORDABILITY
1

# BAG SHARING *pizza*

AFFORDABILITY 1

1 Put the flour, salt, sugar, yeast and 2 tablespoons of the oil in a bowl. Add the measured water and mix with a round-bladed knife to make a soft dough.

2 Turn out on to a floured surface and knead for 10 minutes until the dough is smooth and elastic.

3 Put in a large, lightly oiled bowl, cover with clingfilm and leave to rise in a warm place for about 30-40 minutes until risen to twice the size.

4 While proving, heat another 2 tablespoons of the oil in a frying pan and fry the fennel for 6-8 minutes until golden. Push to one side of the pan, add the fennel seeds, if using, and the asparagus and fry for a further 2 minutes.

5 Turn the dough out on to a floured surface and roll out to a rectangle measuring about 38 × 32 cm (15 × 12½ inches), or the size of your largest baking sheet. Place the dough on the baking sheet and spread the vegan pesto over the pizza, leaving the edges clear. Scatter the fennel and asparagus over the pizza with the artichokes and peas. Bake for 18-20 minutes in a preheated oven, 240°C (475°F), Gas Mark 9, until the dough is risen and golden.

6 Drizzle with the remaining oil and a squeeze of lemon or lime juice. Scatter with basil leaves and serve, cut into squares.

350 g (12 oz) strong white bread flour, plus extra for dusting
1 teaspoon salt
1 teaspoon caster sugar
2 teaspoons fast-action dried yeast
6 tablespoons olive oil
250 ml (8 fl oz) lukewarm water
1 large fennel bulb, thinly sliced
1 teaspoon fennel seeds (optional)
200 g (7 oz) asparagus, trimmed and halved lengthways
100 g (3½ oz) vegan pesto (with tofu)
280 g (9 oz) jar artichoke hearts, drained
100 g (3½ oz) fresh or frozen peas
squeeze of lemon or lime juice
fresh basil leaves, to garnish

Serves **4-5**
Prep time **30 minutes, plus proving**
Cooking time **30 minutes**

# BUBBLE & SQUEAK

AFFORDABILITY
1

1 Mix the potato, red cabbage, onion, flour, soya milk and Dijon mustard together in a large bowl, season with salt and pepper, and form into 4 patties.

2 Heat the coconut oil in a nonstick frying pan, then fry the patties over a medium heat until golden brown on both sides.

3 Serve with hot baked beans, grilled tomatoes and mushrooms or scrambled tofu.

2 tablespoons mashed or baked potato
2 tablespoons finely chopped red cabbage
1 small onion, chopped
2 tablespoons self-raising wholemeal flour
1 tablespoon soya milk
1 teaspoon vegan Dijon mustard
salt and pepper
1 tablespoon coconut oil, for frying

Serves **2**
Prep time **5 minutes**
Cooking time **5 minutes**

## STUDENT TIP

**SEPARATE UTENSILS** If you don't like using pans, knives and chopping boards that have been in contact with meat, keep a separate set of clearly marked kitchen equipment for your own use. If you have a lot of housemates, a plastic box in your room might be the best option.

# SMOKY TOFU
## & POTATO HASH

1  Cook the potatoes in boiling, lightly salted water for
   10 minutes until tender. Drain thoroughly.

2  Drain the tofu of any liquid and squeeze between layers of
   kitchen paper until you've removed as much of the moisture
   as you can. Sprinkle the paprika, bouillon powder and flour
   on a plate. Tear the tofu into pieces and add to the plate.
   Lightly dust with the flour mixture.

3  Combine the tomato ketchup, tomato purée and measured
   water in a jug.

4  Heat 1 tablespoon of the oil in a frying pan and fry the
   leek and onion for 5 minutes, stirring until softened. Add
   the remaining oil, tofu and potatoes and fry for another
   2-3 minutes. Tip in the tomato liquid, cherry tomatoes and
   spinach and heat through for a couple of minutes, stirring
   until the spinach has wilted. Serve immediately.

2 medium baking potatoes, cut
  into small chunks
200 g (7 oz) tofu
½ teaspoon smoked paprika
½ teaspoon vegan bouillon
  powder
1 teaspoon plain flour
2 tablespoons tomato ketchup
1 tablespoon tomato purée
100 ml (3½ fl oz) water
2 tablespoons vegetable oil
1 small leek, thinly sliced
1 onion, thinly sliced
8-10 cherry tomatoes, halved
100 g (3½ oz) baby spinach

Serves **2**
Prep time **10 minutes**
Cooking time **20 minutes**

AFFORDABILITY
1

# TOMATO & MUSHROOM RAGOUT
## on sourdough

1 Heat 1 tablespoon of the oil in a frying pan and fry the onion for 3 minutes until softened. Add the mushrooms and fry for about 5 minutes until the juices have evaporated and the mushrooms are beginning to colour.

2 Stir in the sun-dried tomatoes, cherry tomatoes and half the basil and season with salt and pepper.

3 Toast the bread slices, rub with the cut sides of the garlic and place on serving plates.

4 Drizzle with the remaining oil and spoon the sauce on top. Serve scattered with the remaining basil leaves.

2 tablespoons olive oil
1 red onion, chopped
200 g (7 oz) chestnut mushrooms, roughly chopped
50 g (2 oz) sun-dried tomatoes in oil, drained and chopped
8 cherry tomatoes, quartered
10 g (¼ oz) basil leaves, roughly torn
2 slices of sourdough bread
1 garlic clove, halved
salt and pepper

Serves **2**
Prep time **10 minutes**
Cooking time **10 minutes**

# FLASH-IN-THE-PAN
# RATATOUILLE

1 Heat the oil in a large pan until very hot and stir-fry all of the vegetables, except the chopped tomatoes, for a few minutes. Add the tomatoes, balsamic vinegar and sugar, season and stir well. Cover tightly and simmer for 15 minutes until the vegetables are cooked.

2 Remove from the heat, scatter over the olives and torn basil leaves and serve.

100 ml (3½ fl oz) olive oil
2 onions, chopped
1 aubergine, cut into 1.5 cm (¾ inch) cubes
2 large courgettes, cut into 1.5 cm (¾ inch) cubes
1 red pepper, cored, deseeded and cut into 1.5 cm (¾ inch) pieces
1 yellow pepper, cored, deseeded and cut into 1.5 cm (¾ inch) pieces
2 garlic cloves, crushed
1 × 400 g (14 oz) can chopped tomatoes
2–3 tablespoons balsamic vinegar
1 teaspoon soft brown sugar
10–12 black olives, pitted
salt and pepper
torn basil leaves, to garnish

Serves **4**
Prep time **10 minutes**
Cooking time **20 minutes**

AFFORDABILITY
1

# CURRIED
# CABBAGE
# & CARROT
# *Stir-fry*

1 tablespoon groundnut oil
4 shallots, finely chopped
2 teaspoons peeled and finely
  grated fresh root ginger
2 teaspoons finely grated garlic
2 fresh long green chillies, halved
  lengthways
2 teaspoons cumin seeds
1 teaspoon ground turmeric
1 teaspoon coriander seeds,
  crushed
1 large carrot, coarsely grated
300 g (10 oz) green or white
  cabbage, finely shredded
1 tablespoon curry powder
salt and pepper

Serves **4**
Prep time **10 minutes**
Cooking time **about 15 minutes**

**1** Heat the oil in a large nonstick wok or frying pan over a low heat. Add the shallots, ginger, garlic and chillies and stir-fry for 2–3 minutes until the shallots have softened. Add the cumin seeds, turmeric and crushed coriander seeds and stir-fry for 1 minute.

**2** Increase the heat to high and add the carrot and cabbage, tossing well to coat in the spice mixture. Add the curry powder and season to taste.

**3** Cover the pan and cook over a medium-low heat for 10 minutes, stirring occasionally.

**4** Remove from the heat and serve immediately with steamed rice.

AFFORDABILITY
1

# STIR-FRIED VEGETABLE RICE

1 Heat the oil in a large, nonstick wok and add the spring onions, garlic and ginger. Stir-fry for 4-5 minutes and then add the red pepper, carrot and peas. Stir-fry over a high heat for 3-4 minutes.

2 Stir in the rice, soy and sweet chilli sauces and stir-fry for 3-4 minutes, or until the rice is heated through and piping hot.

3 Remove from the heat and serve immediately, garnished with the chopped herbs.

2 tablespoons sunflower oil
6 spring onions, cut diagonally into 2.5 cm (1 inch) lengths
2 garlic cloves, crushed
1 teaspoon finely grated fresh root ginger
1 red pepper, cored, deseeded and finely chopped
1 carrot, peeled and finely diced
300 g (10 oz) peas
500 g (1 lb 2 oz) cooked, white long-grain rice
1 tablespoon dark soy sauce
1 tablespoon sweet chilli sauce

**To garnish**
coriander leaves, roughly chopped
mint leaves, roughly chopped

Serves **4**
Prep time **10 minutes**
Cooking time **15 minutes**

AFFORDABILITY 1

# CARROT & PEA PILAF

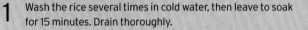

275 g (9 oz) basmati rice
4 tablespoons sunflower oil
1 cinnamon stick
2 teaspoons cumin seeds
2 cloves
4 cardamom pods, lightly bruised
8 black peppercorns
1 large carrot, peeled and coarsely grated
200 g (7 oz) frozen peas
500 ml (18 fl oz) hot water
salt and pepper

.....................................

Serves **4**
Prep time **20 minutes,
  plus soaking and standing**
Cooking time **about 15 minutes**

.....................................

1 Wash the rice several times in cold water, then leave to soak for 15 minutes. Drain thoroughly.

2 Heat the oil in a heavy-based saucepan and add the spices. Stir-fry for 2-3 minutes and then add the carrot and peas. Stir-fry for a further 2-3 minutes and then add the rice. Stir and pour in the measured hot water. Season well.

3 Bring to the boil, cover tightly, reduce the heat and simmer gently for 10 minutes. Do not lift the lid, as the steam is required for the cooking process.

4 Remove the pan from the heat and leave the rice to stand, covered and undisturbed, for 8-10 minutes. Fluff up the grains with a fork and serve immediately.

# Asian-style RISOTTO

AFFORDABILITY **2**

1  Bring the stock, soy sauce and mirin to a simmer in a saucepan. Meanwhile, heat 2 tablespoons of the sunflower oil and the sesame oil in a separate saucepan, add the spring onions, garlic and ginger and cook over a high heat, stirring, for 1 minute. Stir in the rice and lime leaves and cook over a low heat for 1 minute until glossy.

2  Stir 150 ml (¼ pint) of the stock mixture into the rice and simmer, stirring, until it is almost all absorbed. Add the stock, a little at a time, and simmer, stirring, until all but a ladleful has been absorbed. Meanwhile, slice all but a few of the mushrooms. Heat the remaining oil in a frying pan, add the mushrooms and cook over a medium heat, stirring frequently, for 5 minutes until golden.

3  Add the coriander to the risotto with the sliced mushrooms and the remaining stock. Simmer, stirring frequently, until almost all the stock is absorbed and the rice is tender and cooked through. Serve garnished with the whole mushrooms and coriander sprigs.

1.2 litres (2 pints) vegetable stock (see page 219)
1 tablespoon dark soy sauce
2 tablespoons mirin
3 tablespoons sunflower oil
1 tablespoon sesame oil
bunch of spring onions, thickly sliced
2 garlic cloves, chopped
2.5 cm (1 inch) piece of fresh root ginger, peeled and grated
375 g (13 oz) Arborio rice
6 kaffir lime leaves
250 g (8 oz) shiitake mushrooms, wiped and stalks discarded
15 g (½ oz) chopped coriander, plus extra sprigs to garnish

Serves **4**
Preparation time **15 minutes**
Cooking time **25 minutes**

## STUDENT TIP

**BUY IN BULK** Dry goods, cans and multipacks are all good items to buy on special offer, as they'll keep for ages. Find a spare cupboard or clear some space under your bed to store your extra groceries.

# GINGER, COCONUT & LIME LEAF
## *Rice*

250 g (8 oz) jasmine rice
2 teaspoons chopped fresh root ginger
300 ml (½ pint) coconut milk
6 kaffir lime leaves, bashed
1 lemon grass stalk, halved and bruised
1 teaspoon salt
250 ml (8 fl oz) water

Serves **4**
Prep time **10 minutes, plus standing**
Cooking time **15 minutes**

1 Place the rice in a sieve and rinse in cold water until the water runs clear. Drain and shake well.

2 Combine the rice with all the remaining ingredients in a saucepan with a tight-fitting lid. Bring to the boil, cover with the lid and cook over a low heat for 10 minutes.

3 Remove from the heat and leave to stand, covered and without stirring, for 10 minutes. Fluff up with a fork before serving.

**VARIATION**
For cardamom & lemon rice, rinse and drain 250 g (8 oz) basmati rice as above. Heat 1 tablespoon of sunflower oil in a large saucepan with a tight-fitting lid, add 1 chopped onion and cook gently for 2–3 minutes until softened. Stir in 6 crushed cardamom pods and the rice and stir-fry for 2–3 minutes, then pour over 475 ml (16 fl oz) boiling water. Season with salt and stir well, cover with the lid and cook over a low heat for 10 minutes. Remove from the heat and stir in the juice of 2 lemons. Leave to stand, covered and without stirring, for 10 minutes. Fluff up with a fork before serving.

# SPICED RICE
## *with Lentils*

1. Wash the lentils and rice several times in cold water. Drain thoroughly.

2. Heat the oil in a heavy-based saucepan and add the onion. Stir-fry for 6-8 minutes over a medium heat and then add the spices.

3. Continue to stir-fry for 2-3 minutes, then add the rice and lentils. Stir-fry for another 2-3 minutes, then add the stock, tomatoes and fresh coriander. Season well and bring to the boil. Reduce the heat, cover tightly and simmer for 10 minutes.

4. Remove the pan from the heat and allow to stand undisturbed for another 10 minutes. Transfer to a serving dish and garnish with crispy fried onions.

5. Serve immediately with pickles and natural soya yogurt, if liked.

125 g (4 oz) red split lentils
225 g (7½ oz) basmati rice
3 tablespoons sunflower oil
1 onion, finely chopped
1 teaspoon ground turmeric
1 tablespoon cumin seeds
1 dried red chilli
1 cinnamon stick
3 cloves
3 cardamom pods, lightly bruised
500 ml (17 fl oz) vegetable stock
  (see page 219)
8 cherry tomatoes, halved
6 tablespoons finely chopped
  coriander leaves
salt and pepper
crispy fried onions, to garnish

Serves **4**
Prep time **20 minutes,
  plus standing**
Cooking time **20-25 minutes**

AFFORDABILITY

# BOOSTER SNACKS

It's not always possible to plan for three healthy meals every day – deadlines, empty cupboards and late nights are common reasons for coming home and slumping on the sofa with a couple of rounds of toast, rather than a nutritious stir-fry or salad. However, there's a wide selection of natural snacks that you can nibble on during the day to give you an energy boost and bolster your vitamin intake, so that the odd days of unhealthy main meals won't take the edge off your energy levels.

Buy dried ingredients in bulk for better value, and split them into handy portions that you can drop into your bag before you leave the house.

### NUTS
Nutritious, healthy and long-lasting, nuts are the ultimate vegan snack. Just a handful will give you an instant energy boost and keep you going until your next meal. Cashew nuts are particularly beneficial for vegans, as they're high in zinc and iron, while pistachios contain valuable antioxidants and a high level of potassium.

### BLUEBERRIES
Packed full of vitamins, fibre and antioxidants, these little berries are the perfect mid-morning snack. You can also sprinkle a handful over cereal or porridge, or keep them in the freezer and use for smoothies.

### SEEDS
By buying a few essential seeds – pumpkin, sunflower, chia – you can make your own seed mix to nibble on between lectures. You can also sprinkle them over salads, add them to flapjacks, cakes and breakfast bars, and toast or grind them for bulking up main meals.

### SEAWEED
Full of iodine, crispy seaweed makes a great nutritious snack. You can buy different varieties of seaweed in Asian grocers and supermarkets, but always check the packaging to make sure it's a vegan product – some of the seasonings may contain non-vegan ingredients.

### POPCORN
If you fancy a crispy snack, reach for the popcorn, rather than the crisps. But with shop-bought popcorn the salt and flavourings that are added outweigh the nutritional benefits. Luckily it's easy to make it yourself (and so much cheaper) – you'll be getting higher levels of protein and fibre, and you know exactly what you're adding in terms of flavour. A little salt mixed with a pinch of chilli flakes is a good combination.

# *Hot & Smoky* HUMMUS

400 g (14 oz) can cooked
   chickpeas, drained and rinsed
3 tablespoons lemon juice
1 large garlic clove, crushed
2 tablespoons light tahini
1 tablespoon hot smoked paprika,
   plus extra for sprinkling
½ teaspoon ground cumin
150 ml (¼ pint) extra virgin olive
   oil, plus extra for drizzling
2 tablespoons sesame seeds
salt and pepper

**To serve**
4 sheets of Lebanese or Turkish
   flatbread
crunchy raw vegetables (optional)

Serves **4**
Prep time **12 minutes**
Cooking time **20 minutes**

1 Put all the ingredients except the olive oil and sesame seeds in a food processor and blend until smooth. With the machine still running, very slowly drizzle the olive oil into the chickpea paste until it is completely incorporated. Season with salt and pepper and scrape into a small dish.

2 Heat a dry, non-stick frying pan and toast the sesame seeds over a moderately low heat, moving them quickly around the pan until they are golden brown.

3 Stir most of the sesame seeds into the hummus and sprinkle the rest over the top.

4 Wrap the flatbread in foil and heat in a preheated oven, 160°C (325°F), Gas Mark 3, for 20 minutes until warmed through.

5 Drizzle the hummus with olive oil, sprinkle with paprika and serve with the warm flatbread and crunchy vegetables, if liked.

AFFORDABILITY
1

# RED PEPPER & AUBERGINE
# HUMMUS

1 Preheat the oven to 190°C (375°F), Gas Mark 5. Arrange the red pepper, garlic cloves and aubergine in a single layer in a large roasting tin. Drizzle with the chilli oil, sprinkle with the fennel seeds, if using, and season with salt and pepper. Roast for 35-40 minutes, or until softened and golden. Allow the vegetables to cool, but do not turn the oven off.

2 Squeeze the soft garlic out of its skin and put in a food processor or blender with the roasted vegetables, three-quarters of the chickpeas and the tahini. Blend until almost smooth, season with salt and pepper and then spoon into a serving bowl. Leave to cool and cover.

3 Cut the pitta breads into 2.5 cm (1 inch) strips and put in a large bowl. Spray with a little olive oil and toss with the paprika and a little salt until well coated. Spread out in a single layer on a baking sheet. Toast in the oven for 10-12 minutes, or until crisp.

4 Sprinkle the hummus with the remaining chickpeas and toasted sesame seeds and drizzle with 1-2 tablespoons chilli oil. Serve with the toasted pitta breads.

1 red pepper, cored, deseeded and quartered
3 garlic cloves, unpeeled and lightly crushed
1 aubergine, trimmed and cut into large chunks
1 tablespoon chilli oil, plus extra to serve
½ tablespoon fennel seeds (optional)
400 g (14 oz) can chickpeas, drained and rinsed
1 tablespoon tahini
1 teaspoon sesame seeds, lightly toasted
salt and pepper

**To serve**
4 wholemeal pitta breads
olive oil spray
1 teaspoon paprika
salt

Serves **4-6**
Prep time **10 minutes,** plus cooling
Cooking time **50 minutes**

AFFORDABILITY 1

# FENNEL, APPLE & RED CABBAGE *Slaw*

AFFORDABILITY 1

¼ red cabbage, shredded
1 fennel bulb, trimmed and thinly sliced
1 dessert apple, cored and thinly sliced
1 small red onion, thinly sliced
1 celery stick, sliced
2 tablespoons sunflower seeds
2 tablespoons pumpkin seeds
5 tablespoons vegan mayonnaise or Soyannaise (see page 218)
1 tablespoon lemon juice
1 teaspoon vegan Dijon mustard
small handful of flat leaf parsley, roughly chopped
salt and pepper

Serves **4**
Prep time **20 minutes**

1 Put the cabbage in a large bowl, add the fennel, apple, onion, celery and sunflower and pumpkin seeds and toss well to combine.

2 Mix the mayonnaise, lemon juice and mustard together in a small bowl and season with salt and pepper.

3 Add to the cabbage mixture with the parsley and gently toss together to coat all the ingredients in the dressing.

## STUDENT TIP

**PAY BY CASH** Carrying cash, rather than cards, to the supermarket can really help with budgeting. You'll have to buy within your means, shop cannily and add up your purchases as you go. And, if you do manage to bag a few bargains, you can spend the extra on a treat or two.

# SEEDED CHIPS
## WITH RED PEPPER DIP

450 g (1 lb) sweet potatoes, peeled
  and cut into wedges
450 g (1 lb) white potatoes, peeled
  and cut into wedges
4 tablespoons olive oil
1 tablespoon poppy seeds
1 tablespoon sesame seeds
1 teaspoon dried chilli flakes
1 large red pepper, cored,
  deseeded and cut into 4 wedges
2 tomatoes, halved
½ teaspoon smoked paprika
3 tablespoons chopped coriander
salt and pepper

Serves **4**
Prep time **20 minutes**
Cooking time **35 minutes**

**1** Preheat the oven to 200°C (400°F), Gas Mark 6 . Drizzle the sweet potato and white potato wedges with 3 tablespoons of the olive oil in a large roasting tin and toss well, then scatter over the poppy and sesame seeds and chilli flakes and toss again.

**2** Season generously with salt and pepper and roast in the top of the oven for 35 minutes until golden.

**3** Meanwhile, put the pepper wedges and tomatoes in a smaller roasting tin, then drizzle with the remaining olive oil and toss well. Roast on a lower shelf in the oven for 25 minutes until softened and lightly charred in places. Leave to cool.

**4** Transfer the roasted pepper and tomatoes to a food processor, season generously with salt and pepper and add the smoked paprika. Process until almost smooth but with a little texture still remaining.

**5** Spoon into a small serving bowl and place in the centre of a serving platter. Arrange the roasted potato wedges on the platter, scatter with the chopped coriander and serve.

AFFORDABILITY
**1**

# AUBERGINE DIP
## & crispy tortillas

1. Preheat the oven to 220°C (425°F), Gas Mark 7. Put the aubergine in a bowl with 6 tablespoons of the extra virgin olive oil and toss well.

2. Transfer to a large roasting tin and roast for 25 minutes until soft and lightly charred in places. Leave to cool.

3. Transfer the aubergine to a food processor and add the garlic, ¼ teaspoon of the smoked paprika, the tahini, lemon juice, half the chopped parsley and plenty of salt and pepper. Process until smooth, then transfer to a serving bowl.

4. Mix the remaining extra virgin olive oil with the remaining paprika and use it to swirl over the top of the dip. Scatter with the remaining chopped parsley.

5. Brush each tortilla triangle lightly with the olive oil and spread them evenly across 1 or 2 large baking sheets. Sprinkle with the salt and cook them under a preheated medium grill for 1-2 minutes until lightly crisp and golden. Arrange the tortillas around the dip bowl and serve.

1 large aubergine, about 750 g (1½ lb), trimmed and cut into thick chunks
8 tablespoons extra virgin olive oil
1 garlic clove, crushed
½ teaspoon smoked paprika
3 tablespoons tahini
juice of 1 lemon
1 tablespoon chopped flat leaf parsley
salt and pepper

**Tortillas**
6 mini flour tortillas, cut into triangles
1 tablespoon olive oil
1 teaspoon sea salt flakes

Serves **6**
Prep time **15 minutes, plus cooling**
Cooking time **30 minutes**

AFFORDABILITY
1

# THE MAIN EVENT

POTATO, ROSEMARY
& ONION PIE

QUICK VEGETABLE MOLE

TAGLIATELLE WITH PUMPKIN
& SAGE

# SPICED ONION PANCAKES
## WITH RED LENTIL & CHICKPEA DAHL

3 tablespoons vegetable oil, plus extra for shallow-frying
4 garlic cloves, crushed
2 tablespoons curry leaves
3 large onions, very thinly sliced
3 carrots, cut into small dice
200 g (7 oz) red lentils, rinsed
25 g (1 oz) fresh root ginger, finely chopped
1 teaspoon ground turmeric
2 teaspoons ground cumin
1 red chilli, deseeded and finely chopped
1 litre (1¾ pints) vegetable stock (see page 219)
400 g (14 oz) can chickpeas
50 g (2 oz) plain flour
10 g (¼ oz) coriander, chopped
salt and pepper

Serves **4**
Prep time **25 minutes**
Cooking time **45 minutes**

1 Heat the 3 tablespoons of oil in a large shallow pan and fry the garlic and curry leaves for 30 seconds. Lift out with a slotted spoon on to a plate.

2 To make the dahl, tip a third of the sliced onions into the oil and fry gently for 5 minutes. Add the carrots, red lentils, ginger, turmeric, cumin, chilli and stock. Bring to a simmer and cover with a lid. Cook very gently for 30 minutes until the lentils are tender and turning mushy.

3 Drain the chickpeas, reserving the liquid. Measure 100 ml (3½ fl oz) of the chickpea liquid into a bowl and whisk using a hand-held electric whisk or balloon whisk until foamy. Sprinkle in the flour and stir in to make a paste. Add the remaining onions, coriander and a little salt and pepper and mix well.

4 Stir the chickpeas, curry leaves and garlic into the dahl and heat through gently while preparing the onion pancakes, adding a dash of hot water if the dahl has over thickened.

5 Pour a thin film of oil into a frying pan and heat. Add spoonfuls of the onion mixture and flatten down gently. Cook for about 2 minutes until golden on the underside. Flip over and cook for another 1–2 minutes. Drain on kitchen paper while you fry any remaining onion batter. Serve with the dahl.

# EASY DOSA
## *with mixed bean sambar*

1 Mix the rice flour, fennel seeds, plain flour, salt and measured cold water to make the dosa batter. Leave to stand for about 2 hours.

2 For the sambar, heat the oil in a large saucepan and gently fry the onions, fennel and carrots for 10 minutes. Add the garlic and fry for a further 2 minutes. Stir in the tomatoes, curry paste, stock, tomato purée and turmeric and bring to a simmer. Cover with a lid and cook gently for 20 minutes.

3 Add the runner beans and peas, cover and cook for a further 10 minutes until the vegetables are completely tender.

4 Meanwhile, fry the dosa. Heat a little oil in a small frying pan or crepe pan until just smoking. Give the dosa batter a stir and pour a small ladleful into the pan, spreading it slightly with the base of the ladle. Cook until set and pale golden on the underside. Turn and briefly cook the other side.

5 Transfer to a plate and keep warm while cooking the remaining batter in the same way, re-oiling the pan when necessary. If the pan is large enough you'll be able to cook 2 or 3 at the same time.

6 Transfer the sambar to serving bowls, sprinkle with the coriander and serve with the warm dosa.

250 g (8 oz) rice flour
2 teaspoons fennel seeds
25 g (1 oz) plain flour
1½ teaspoons salt
400 ml (14 fl oz) cold water
vegetable oil, for frying

**Sambar**
2 tablespoons vegetable oil
2 large onions, chopped
1 fennel bulb, roughly chopped
3 carrots, roughly chopped
4 garlic cloves, chopped
200 g (7 oz) can chopped
   tomatoes
2-3 tablespoons vegan mild curry
   paste
500 ml (1 pint) vegetable stock
   (see page 219)
2 tablespoons tomato purée
1 teaspoon ground turmeric
200 g (7 oz) runner beans,
   trimmed and thinly sliced
100 g (3½ oz) fresh or frozen peas
15 g (½ oz) coriander, chopped

Serves **4**
Prep time **30 minutes,**
   **plus standing**
Cooking time **50 minutes**

AFFORDABILITY
1

# COURGETTES
## STUFFED WITH WALNUT AND LENTIL PÂTÉ

4 courgettes
1 tablespoon avocado or olive oil
1 tablespoon soy sauce

**Pâté**
125 g (4 oz) red lentils
½ onion, chopped
1 garlic clove, chopped
250 ml (8 fl oz) vegetable stock
  (see page 219)
25 g (1 oz) shelled walnuts,
  chopped
1 teaspoon cider vinegar
1 teaspoon yeast extract
2 teaspoons chopped dates
1 tablespoon rapeseed oil
1 teaspoon soya milk
1 teaspoon chopped thyme

Serves **4**
Prep time **15 minutes**
Cooking time **45-50 minutes**

1 First make the pâté. Fill a medium saucepan with cold water, add the lentils and bring to the boil.

2 Drain the lentils, rinse under running cold water, then return them to the saucepan. Add the onion, garlic and vegetable stock and bring to the boil, then simmer for 20 minutes.

3 Drain the lentils again, then stir in all the remaining pâté ingredients. Transfer the mixture to a food processor or liquidizer and blend until smooth.

4 Slice a thin sliver from the bottom of the courgettes so that they sit level on a plate. Cut a rectangle almost the length and width of the courgettes through the skin on the top side. Carefully remove the rectangle of skin, then scoop out the flesh using a teaspoon. (Freeze the flesh to use later in another recipe.)

5 Mix together the avocado or olive oil and soy sauce, then brush the cut surfaces of the courgettes with it. Bake for about 15 minutes in a preheated oven, 180°C (350°F), Gas Mark 4. Remove the courgettes from the oven, fill with the lentil pâté and return to the oven for 5-10 minutes to heat through.

6 Serve with a mixed salad, chutney and warm oat cakes.

# Stuffed
# MUSHROOMS

2 large, flat field mushrooms
2 tablespoons olive oil, plus extra
  for oiling
2 spring onions, chopped
½ red pepper, cored, deseeded
  and chopped
1 small courgette, chopped
4 olives, pitted and chopped
2 tablespoons porridge oats
1 tablespoon chopped basil
1 tablespoon soy sauce
1 tablespoon lime juice
salt and pepper
mixed salad leaves, to serve

Serves **2**
Prep time **5 minutes**
Cooking time **20-25 minutes**

1 Preheat the oven to 180°C (350°F), Gas Mark 4. Remove the mushroom stalks and chop them.

2 Heat the oil in a small saucepan and gently fry the mushroom stalks, spring onions, red pepper, courgette, olives and oats until the oats are golden. Stir in the basil, soy sauce and lime juice.

3 Oil the mushroom caps and place them on a baking sheet. Spoon the oat mixture on to the mushrooms, season with salt and pepper, and bake for 15-20 minutes, until the caps start to soften.

4 Serve the hot mushrooms immediately on a bed of mixed salad leaves.

AFFORDABILITY
1

# Turkish Stuffed BUTTERNUT SQUASH

1 Sit the squash halves, cut-side up, in a large roasting tin, brush each with 1 tablespoon of oil and season with salt and pepper. Roast in a preheated oven, 220°C (425°F), Gas Mark 7, for 45 minutes until lightly charred on top.

2 Meanwhile, heat the oil for the filling in a large, heavy-based frying pan, add the onion, garlic and cumin and cook over a medium-high heat, stirring occasionally, for 4-5 minutes until beginning to soften. Add the tomatoes, parsley, oregano and sun-dried tomato purée and cook, stirring occasionally, for a further 5 minutes. Season well with salt and pepper.

3 Divide the filling between the cavities of the roasted squash halves and scatter with the cumin seeds. Reduce the oven temperature to 180°C (350°F), Gas Mark 4, and roast the stuffed squash for 20 minutes, or until the filling is soft and golden in places. Serve with a simple rocket salad, if liked.

2 butternut squash, halved and deseeded
4 tablespoons olive oil
salt and pepper

**Filling**
3 tablespoons olive oil
1 large onion, finely chopped
1 garlic clove, thinly sliced
1 teaspoon ground cumin
450 g (1 lb) tomatoes, roughly chopped
4 tablespoons chopped flat leaf parsley
1 tablespoon chopped oregano
2 tablespoons sun-dried tomato purée
1 teaspoon cumin seeds
salt and pepper

Serves **4**
Prep time **25 minutes**
Cooking time **1 hour 5 minutes**

# *Herby* QUINOA-STUFFED TOMATOES

50 g (2 oz) quinoa, rinsed and
  drained
4 large beef tomatoes
½ small red onion, finely chopped
75 g (3 oz) roasted peppers from a
  jar, drained and sliced
1 red chilli, deseeded and chopped
2 tablespoons chopped flat leaf
  parsley
2 tablespoon chopped coriander
2 tablespoons sunflower seeds
1 teaspoon sesame oil
1 tablespoon soy sauce, plus extra
  to serve
2 tablespoons olive oil
pepper

Serves **4**
Prep time **20 minutes**
Cooking time **40-50 minutes**

1 Add the quinoa to a saucepan of boiling water, then simmer for 10-12 minutes until tender. Drain, rinse in cold water and drain again.

2 Meanwhile, cut the tops off the tomatoes and hollow out the centres with a teaspoon. Put half the tomato pulp and seeds in a bowl, discarding the rest, and add the onion, peppers, chilli, parsley, coriander and sunflower seeds and mix well.

3 Stir the sesame oil and soy sauce together and pour into the bowl. Mix well, then add the quinoa and mix again. Season with pepper; the soy sauce is salty, so you won't need to add extra salt.

4 Sit the tomato shells on a baking tray. Spoon the quinoa mixture into the tomatoes, drizzle with the olive oil and bake in a preheated oven, 190°C (375°F), Gas Mark 5, for 30-35 minutes until the tomatoes are tender.

# TEMPEH & QUINOA SUPERFOOD BOWL

200 g (7 oz) black, red or white
  quinoa
300 ml (½ pint) water
1 teaspoon vegan bouillon powder
150 g (5 oz) sugar snap peas or
  mangetout, sliced diagonally
100 g (3½ oz) kale, shredded
200 g (7 oz) tempeh
1 tablespoon olive oil
3 tablespoons pumpkin seeds
4 tablespoons chopped chives
50 g (2 oz) almonds, cashew nuts
  or peanuts
50 g (2 oz) sultanas

**Dressing**
50 g (2 oz) tahini
1 garlic clove, crushed
100 g (3½ oz) soya yogurt
2 teaspoons caster sugar
1 teaspoon vegan wine vinegar
  or lemon juice
salt and pepper

Serves **2-3**
Prep time **10 minutes**
Cooking time **20 minutes**

1 Put the quinoa in a saucepan with the measured water and the bouillon powder. Cook very gently until the quinoa is tender and the liquid is absorbed, about 10 minutes. Place the sugar snaps or mangetout and kale on top. Cover with a lid and cook gently for a further 5 minutes until the vegetables are tender. Turn into a bowl.

2 Place the tempeh between several sheets of kitchen paper and squeeze out the moisture. Heat the oil in a frying pan and fry the tempeh on both sides until golden, about 3-4 minutes. Add the pumpkin seeds and cook for a further 30 seconds, or until they start to pop. Slice the tempeh and add to the bowl along with the seeds.

3 For the dressing, put all the ingredients in a bowl and beat well with a whisk until thick and smooth. Stir the chives, nuts and sultanas into the salad and serve with spoonfuls of the dressing.

AFFORDABILITY 2

# PEA & MINT PESTO
# FETTUCCINE

250 g (8 oz) dried egg-free
  fettuccine
250 g (8 oz) frozen peas,
  defrosted
1 garlic clove, roughly chopped
1 teaspoon wasabi
5 tablespoons mint leaves
6 tablespoons olive oil
2 tablespoons pine nuts
150 ml (¼ pint) water
salt and pepper
mint leaves, to garnish

Serves **4**
Prep time **20 minutes**
Cooking time **10-12 minutes**

1 Cook the fettuccine in a large saucepan of lightly salted boiling water for 8-10 minutes until just tender.

2 Meanwhile, blend together the peas, garlic, wasabi, mint, oil, pine nuts and the measured water in a blender or food processor until well combined. Season with plenty of salt and pepper.

3 Drain the pasta well and return to the pan with the pea pesto. Toss over a gentle heat for 2-3 minutes until piping hot.

4 Sprinkle with the mint leaves and serve immediately in warmed serving bowls with crusty bread.

**VARIATION**

For basil pesto with fettuccine, cook 350 g (12 oz) dried egg-free fettuccine as above. Meanwhile, blend together 1 garlic clove, 2 handfuls of basil leaves, 6 tablespoons of olive oil and 3 tablespoons of pine nuts in a blender or food processor until smooth. Season well with salt and pepper. Drain the pasta well and return to the pan with the basil pesto. Toss over a gentle heat for 1-2 minutes until piping hot, then serve immediately in warmed serving bowls.

AFFORDABILITY
2

# PASTA *with* ROMESCO SAUCE

150 g (5 oz) fusilli or penne pasta
50 g (2 oz) vegan white bread
3 tablespoons olive oil
2 pointed red peppers, cored, deseeded and chopped
40 g (1½ oz) flaked almonds
3 tablespoons chopped parsley
1 red chilli, deseeded and finely chopped
2 garlic cloves, finely chopped
1 teaspoon vegan bouillon powder
2 tablespoons tomato purée
2 teaspoons vegan white or red wine vinegar
200 ml (7 fl oz) water
salt and pepper

Serves **2**
Prep time **10 minutes**
Cooking time **20 minutes**

1 Bring a saucepan of salted water to the boil and cook the pasta for about 12 minutes, or until tender.

2 Make coarse breadcrumbs from the bread, either in a food processor or by grating using a box grater.

3 Heat 1 tablespoon of the oil in a frying pan and fry the peppers for 6–8 minutes until softened and beginning to brown. Lift out on to a plate and add the remaining oil, almonds and breadcrumbs to the pan. Fry gently for a couple of minutes, stirring frequently until the crumbs are beginning to brown. Spoon 3 tablespoons of the mixture on to a plate, stir in the parsley and set aside.

4 Return the peppers to the pan with the chilli, garlic, bouillon powder, tomato purée, vinegar and measured water. Cook, stirring frequently for 5 minutes until thick and pulpy, adding a dash more water if the mixture becomes very dry.

5 Drain the pasta and return to the saucepan. Add the pepper sauce and mix well to combine. Transfer to serving plates and scatter the parsley crumbs on top.

# *Pasta*
## WITH TOMATO & BASIL SAUCE

1  Cook the pasta in a large saucepan of salted boiling water according to the packet instructions.

2  Meanwhile, heat 1 tablespoon of the oil in a frying pan, add the garlic and cook over a low heat for 1 minute. As soon as the garlic begins to change colour, remove the pan from the heat and add the remaining oil.

3  Drain the pasta and return to the pan. Add the garlic oil with the tomatoes and basil. Season to taste with salt and pepper and toss well to mix. Serve immediately.

400 g (14 oz) dried spaghetti
5 tablespoons olive oil
5 garlic cloves, finely chopped
6 vine-ripened tomatoes,
   deseeded and chopped
25 g (1 oz) basil leaves
salt and pepper

Serves **4**
Prep time **10 minutes**
Cooking time **10 minutes**

# CHICKPEA
## MINESTRONE
## WITH ROCKET

1 Heat the oil in a large, deep saucepan, add the onion and cook over a medium-high heat for 3–4 minutes until beginning to soften. Add the garlic and cook, stirring, for 1 minute.

2 Add the chickpeas, green beans and tomatoes to the pan and stir well, then stir in the stock, tomato juice and pasta. Bring to the boil, then cover and simmer for 15 minutes until the pasta is tender.

3 Remove the lid and continue to cook for a further 10 minutes, adding three-quarters of the rocket and the parsley just before the end of cooking and stirring through. Season generously with salt and pepper.

4 Serve in warmed serving bowls with the remaining rocket scattered over to garnish, along with warm crusty wholemeal bread.

2 tablespoons olive oil
1 red onion, finely chopped
1 garlic clove, sliced
400 g (14 oz) can chickpeas, drained and rinsed
150 g (5 oz) green beans, trimmed and diagonally sliced
200 g (7 oz) cherry tomatoes
900 ml (1½ pints) vegetable stock (see page 219)
300 ml (½ pint) tomato juice
150 g (5 oz) dried wholewheat pasta shapes
70 g (3 oz) wild rocket
6 tablespoons chopped flat leaf parsley
salt and pepper

Serves **4**
Prep time **20 minutes**
Cooking time **30 minutes**

AFFORDABILITY
1

# Caper, Lemon & Chilli
# SPAGHETTI

350 g (12 oz) spelt spaghetti
200 g (7 oz) tenderstem broccoli, cut into chunks
2 tablespoons olive oil
1 small red onion, thinly sliced
1 red chilli, deseeded and chopped
2 tablespoons capers
finely grated zest of 1 lemon and 1 tablespoon juice
2 tablespoons balsamic vinegar
salt and pepper

Serves **4**
Prep time **5 minutes**
Cooking time **12 minutes**

1 Cook the spaghetti in a large saucepan of salted boiling water for 10 minutes, adding the broccoli for the final 3 minutes, or until just tender.

2 Meanwhile, heat the oil in a frying pan, add the onion and chilli and cook over a gentle heat for 2 minutes. Stir in the capers, lemon zest and juice and vinegar, season with salt and pepper and heat through.

3 Drain the spaghetti and broccoli, reserving 1 tablespoon of the cooking water and adding to the caper mixture. Add the drained spaghetti and broccoli to the pan and toss well to combine over the heat. Serve with an extra grinding of black pepper.

**VARIATION**
For artichoke, lemon & mint spaghetti, cook 350 g (12 oz) spaghetti as above, adding 125 g (4 oz) frozen peas for the final 3 minutes until just tender. Meanwhile, heat 2 tablespoons of olive oil in a frying pan, add a drained 290 g (9¾ oz) jar of marinated artichokes in oil and heat through for 1 minute. Stir in the finely grated zest of 1 lemon, 1 tablespoon of lemon juice and 2 tablespoons each of balsamic vinegar and chopped mint and season with salt and pepper. Drain the spaghetti and peas, reserving 1 tablespoon of the cooking water and adding to the artichoke mixture. Add the drained spaghetti and peas to the pan and toss well to combine over the heat. Serve with an extra grinding of pepper.

# CHILLI & AVOCADO
# PASTA BOWL

175 g (6 oz) spinach trottole or
other pasta shapes
1 large ripe avocado
2 tablespoons olive oil
2 spring onions, chopped
½ red chilli, deseeded and finely
chopped
2 tablespoons sweet chilli sauce
1 tomato, diced
small handful coriander, chopped
lime wedges, to serve

Serves **2**
Prep time **10 minutes**
Cooking time **10 minutes**

1 Cook the pasta in boiling, lightly salted water for about 10 minutes, or until tender.

2 Halve and stone the avocado. Scoop one half into a bowl and thoroughly mash with the oil. Beat in the spring onions, chilli, chilli sauce and tomato. Dice the remaining avocado.

3 Drain the pasta and return to the pan. Stir in the avocado sauce and diced avocado. Transfer to serving bowls and scatter with the coriander. Serve with lime wedges for squeezing over.

## STUDENT TIP

**STEAMING GREENS** Get into the habit of steaming rather than boiling vegetables. They will taste better and you won't lose all the valuable nutrients in the cooking water. You don't need an expensive steamer; you can use a metal colander over a pan of simmering water. Pop a lid on top to keep the steam in.

# MIXED MUSHROOM
## *Bolognese*

1. Place the dried mushrooms in a bowl and pour over enough hot water to cover. Leave to soak for 20 minutes.

2. Heat the oil in a large saucepan, add the onion, celery, carrot and garlic and cook over a low heat for 8 minutes, stirring occasionally, until softened. Increase the heat, stir in the fresh mushrooms and cook for 3-4 minutes.

3. Strain the soaked dried mushrooms through a sieve, reserving the liquid. Add the dried mushrooms to the pan.

4. Pour over the wine, bring to the boil and cook until reduced by half. Stir in the reserved soaking liquid, tomatoes, tomato purée, vinegar and oregano, season with salt and pepper and bring to the boil.

5. Reduce the heat, cover and simmer for 40-50 minutes until the sauce is thick and the mushrooms are tender.

6. Meanwhile, cook the spaghetti in a large saucepan of lightly salted boiling water for 8-10 minutes, or according to the packet instructions, until al dente. Drain and serve straight away topped with the mushroom sauce and grated cheese.

25 g (1 oz) dried wild mushrooms
 (eg porcini and chanterelle)
2 tablespoons olive oil
1 large onion, chopped
1 celery stick, finely chopped
1 carrot, finely chopped
2 garlic cloves, crushed
500 g (1 lb 2 oz) mixed
 mushrooms, trimmed and
 roughly chopped
150 ml (¼ pint) vegan red wine
400 g (14 oz) can chopped
 tomatoes
1 tablespoon tomato purée
1 teaspoon balsamic vinegar
2 teaspoons dried oregano
300 g (10 oz) dried spaghetti
salt and pepper
grated Parmesan-style vegan
 cheese, to serve

Serves **4**
Prep time **20 minutes,
 plus soaking**
Cooking time **1-1 ¼ hours**

AFFORDABILITY
3

# TAGLIATELLE
## with Pumpkin & Sage

1  Place the pumpkin into a small roasting tin, add half the olive oil, season and toss to mix well. Roast in a preheated oven, 220°C (425°F), Gas Mark 7, for 15-20 minutes, or until just tender.

2  Meanwhile, bring a large saucepan of salted water to the boil. Cook the pasta according to the packet instructions. Drain, return to the pan, then add the rocket, sage and roasted pumpkin. Mix together over a gentle heat with the remaining olive oil until the rocket has wilted, then serve with a good grating of Parmesan-style vegan cheese, if desired.

875 g (1¾ lb) pumpkin, butternut or winter squash, peeled, deseeded and cut into 1.5 cm (¾ inch) cubes
4 tablespoons olive oil
500 g (1 lb 2 oz) fresh tagliatelle
50 g (2 oz) rocket leaves
8 sage leaves, chopped
salt and pepper

Serves **4**
Prep time **10 minutes**
Cooking time **20 minutes**

AFFORDABILITY

# BUTTERNUT SQUASH & FRIED SAGE
## *Linguini*

**1** Slice the squash across into 2 cm (¾ inch) slices. Discard the seeds and cut away the skin. Chop the flesh into small pieces and scatter in a roasting tin with the onions. Drizzle with 2 tablespoons of the oil and roast in a preheated oven, 200°C (400°F), Gas Mark 6, for 35-40 minutes, turning halfway through cooking, until tender and pale golden.

**2** Heat the remaining oil in a large saucepan and add one sage leaf to see if the oil is hot enough for the sage to sizzle; if necessary heat the oil a little more. Add the remaining leaves and cook for about 30 seconds until crisped and lightly browned. Stir in the garlic and then tip into a small bowl, including the oil.

**3** Wipe out the saucepan, then fill with plenty of water and bring to the boil. Cook the linguini until tender, about 10 minutes. Scoop out a small ladleful or cup of the liquid and drain the pasta.

**4** Return to the pan with the reserved liquid and tip in the roasted vegetables, sage, garlic, oil and cheese. Mix well and pile on to serving plates, sprinkling with extra cheese.

1 medium butternut squash
2 red onions, thinly sliced
4 tablespoons mild olive oil
20 fresh sage leaves
2 garlic cloves, finely chopped
150 g (5 oz) linguini
50 g (2 oz) Cheddar-style vegan cheese, finely grated, plus extra to sprinkle

Serves **2**
Prep time **15 minutes**
Cooking time **40 minutes**

# GNOCCHI
## IN TOMATO & LEEK SAUCE

625 g (1¼ lb) floury potatoes, such as King Edward or Maris Piper, scrubbed
125 g (4 oz) plain flour
salt and pepper

**Sauce**
1 tablespoon olive oil
1 leek, trimmed, cleaned and chopped
1 garlic clove, crushed
4 ripe tomatoes, roughly chopped
1 tablespoon tomato purée
pinch of sugar
small handful of torn basil leaves
salt and pepper

Serves **4**
Prep time **30 minutes**
Cooking time **25 minutes**

**1** Cook the potatoes in their skins in a large saucepan of salted boiling water for about 20 minutes until tender. Drain and leave until cool enough to handle but not cold.

**2** Meanwhile, make the sauce. Heat the oil in a frying pan, add the leek and cook over a medium heat for 5 minutes until tender. Add the garlic and tomatoes and cook for 5 minutes until the tomatoes are soft. Stir in the tomato purée and a little water to make a sauce. Add the sugar, season with salt and pepper and simmer for 3 minutes.

**3** Peel the potatoes and pass them through a potato ricer or mash with a potato masher until smooth. Season with salt and pepper, then knead in the flour to form a dough.

**4** Divide the gnocchi dough into 4 pieces and roll each piece into a thick sausage. Cut into 1.5 cm (¾ inch) pieces and press with the prongs of a fork to mark a ridged pattern.

**5** Cook the gnocchi in a large saucepan of salted boiling water for 1-2 minutes until they float to the surface. Remove from the pan with a slotted spoon and add to the sauce. Add the basil and gently turn the gnocchi to coat in the sauce. Serve with an extra grinding of pepper.

### VARIATION
For fried gnocchi with broccoli & lemon, make the gnocchi as above (or use shop-bought vegan gnocchi). Cook 300 g (10 oz) broccoli, cut into florets, in a saucepan of boiling salted water for 3 minutes until just tender, then drain. Meanwhile, heat 3 tablespoons of olive oil in a large frying pan, add the gnocchi and fry for 8-10 minutes until golden and crisp. Stir in 1 chopped red chilli, 1 crushed garlic clove, the finely grated zest of 1 lemon and the broccoli and heat through for 3 minutes.

# PEARL BARLEY RISOTTO WITH CARROTS

AFFORDABILITY
1

225 g (7½ oz) pearl barley
400 g (14 oz) baby carrots,
  scrubbed
5 tablespoons olive oil
1 large onion, finely chopped
1 large leek, trimmed, cleaned
  and thinly sliced
1 garlic clove, thinly sliced
1 tablespoon thyme leaves
1 teaspoon ground coriander
1.2 litres (2 pints) vegetable stock
  (see page 219), plus extra if
  needed
2 tablespoons chopped flat leaf
  parsley, to garnish
salt and pepper

Serves **4**
Prep time **15 minutes,**
  **plus standing**
Cooking time **25 minutes**

**1** Put the pearl barley in a bowl, pour over enough boiling water to cover and leave to stand for 10 minutes.

**2** Toss the carrots in a shallow roasting tin with 2 tablespoons of the oil until evenly coated, then roast in a preheated oven, 200°C (400°F), Gas Mark 6, for 20 minutes until tender and lightly charred in places.

**3** Meanwhile, heat the remaining oil in a frying pan, add the onion and leek with the garlic and thyme and cook over a medium heat, stirring occasionally, for 4 minutes until soft and pale golden. Stir in the ground coriander and cook for a further 1 minute.

**4** Drain the pearl barley, add to the frying pan with half the stock and bring to the boil. Cover and simmer very gently, stirring occasionally, for about 10 minutes until almost all the stock is absorbed. Add the remaining stock and stir, then cover and simmer gently again until the pearl barley is tender and some of the stock is still left in the pan, adding more stock if necessary.

**5** Add the roasted carrots to the risotto and stir through. Season and serve with warm wholemeal bread.

**VARIATION**
For roasted root vegetable risotto, put 200 g (7 oz) scrubbed baby carrots into a roasting tin with 2 parsnips, peeled and cut into batons, and 225 g (7½ oz) peeled and chopped turnips. Add 3 tablespoons of olive oil and toss. Add 1 tablespoon of chopped rosemary leaves and toss again. Roast in a preheated oven, 200°C (400°F), Gas Mark 6, for 20-25 minutes until lightly charred and tender. Meanwhile, cook the onion, leek and garlic as above, omitting the thyme, then add and cook the pearl barley as above. Fold in the roasted veg and season.

Marino Branch
Brainse Marino
Tel: 8336297

# TOFU
## & VEGETABLE FRIED RICE

AFFORDABILITY
**2**

1  Spray a large nonstick wok or frying pan with cooking spray and heat over a high heat. Add the onion and stir-fry for 1–2 minutes until slightly softened. Add the garlic and chilli and stir-fry for about 1 minute until aromatic.

2  Add the carrot, baby corn, pak choi stems and tomatoes to the pan and stir-fry for about 3 minutes until softened. Transfer to a bowl.

3  Wipe the pan clean with kitchen paper, re-spray with cooking spray and heat over a high heat. Add the cooked rice and stir-fry for about 3–4 minutes until piping hot. Add the pak choi leaves, sweet chilli sauce and soy sauce with the reserved vegetables and toss together briefly until heated through. Remove from the heat and stir in the tofu and herbs. Ladle into warmed bowls and serve.

cooking spray
1 red onion, cut into thin wedges
2 garlic cloves, finely chopped
1 red chilli, deseeded and finely chopped
1 carrot, cut into thin matchsticks
175 g (6 oz) baby corn, diagonally sliced
1 bunch of pak choi, stems and leaves separated
200 g (7 oz) cherry tomatoes, halved
500 g (1 lb 2 oz) freshly cooked long-grain rice, cooled
2 tablespoons sweet chilli sauce
2 tablespoons light soy sauce
200 g (7 oz) firm tofu, drained and cut into bite-sized cubes
large handful of coriander and mint leaves, finely chopped

Serves **4**
Prep time **15 minutes**
Cooking time **15 minutes**

# GINGER & TOFU
## Sweet & Sour

1. Make the tamarind purée, if using. Soak 50 g (2 oz) dried tamarind pulp (about 2 tablespoons) in 200 ml (7 fl oz) boiling water for 4–5 minutes. Mash with a spoon or fork to help it dissolve. Then strain the thick liquid into a small bowl and reserve the fibres in another bowl (use these if you need to strain the liquid again).

2. Heat 5 cm (2 inches) of oil in a wok over a medium heat. Deep-fry the ginger without stirring for 6–8 minutes. Remove the ginger with a slotted spoon, then drain on kitchen paper.

3. Lower the tofu into the oil, in batches, and deep-fry for 5–6 minutes until lightly browned and soft inside. Drain on kitchen paper.

4. Remove most of the oil, leaving 1½ tablespoons in the wok. Stir-fry the garlic over a medium heat for 1–2 minutes, or until lightly browned. Add the sugar, soy sauce, stock or water and tamarind purée or lime juice and stir over a low heat until slightly thickened. Taste and adjust the seasoning. Add the tofu and most of the crispy ginger and mix together.

5. Spoon into 4 warm serving bowls and garnish with the remainder of the crispy ginger.

3 tablespoons tamarind purée or 2 tablespoons lime juice
sunflower oil, for deep-frying
300 g (10 oz) fresh root ginger, finely shredded
500 g (1 lb 2 oz) firm tofu, drained, cut into 1 cm (½ inch) cubes
2 garlic cloves, finely chopped
40 g (1½ oz) coconut, palm or brown sugar
2 tablespoons light soy sauce
2 tablespoons vegetable stock (see page 219) or water

Serves **4**
Prep time **15 minutes**
Cooking time **30–40 minutes**

AFFORDABILITY
2

# Crunchy nut stir-fry
## ON SWEET POTATO & MISO MASH

400 g (14 oz) sweet potatoes, scrubbed and cut into small chunks
2 tablespoons vegetable oil
300 g (10 oz) mixed stir-fry vegetables, including bean sprouts
½ bunch spring onions, chopped
100g (3½ oz) spring greens, shredded
2 tablespoons white or brown miso paste
3 tablespoons rice or almond milk
50 g (2 oz) salted peanuts
1 tablespoon soy sauce
2 teaspoons rice wine vinegar or vegan wine vinegar

Serves **2**
Prep time **10 minutes**
Cooking time **10 minutes**

1 Cook the potatoes in boiling water for 8-10 minutes, or until tender.

2 Meanwhile, heat the oil in a frying pan or wok and add the stir-fry vegetables, spring onions and spring greens. Fry, stirring, for 3-4 minutes until slightly softened.

3 Drain the sweet potatoes and return to the saucepan. Mash well and beat in the miso paste and milk.

4 Spoon the mash on to serving plates and spread out a little with the back of the spoon. Stir the peanuts into the stir-fry and heat through briefly. Turn out on to the mash to serve and drizzle the soy sauce and vinegar on top.

# NOODLE & VEGETABLE
## *Stir-fry*

1 Soak the rice noodles in boiling water for 4 minutes, then rinse in cold water and drain.

2 Heat a wok or large frying pan until very hot, add the coconut oil, then the onion and tofu. Stir briskly to sear on all sides until golden.

3 Pour in the soy sauce and stir to coat the mixture. Reduce the heat and add the remaining ingredients plus the drained noodles, stirring until hot.

4 Transfer the stir-fry to warmed serving bowls, sprinkle with nori flakes and sesame seeds, and serve with a wedge of lime, if liked.

50 g (2 oz) rice noodles
2 teaspoons coconut oil
1 red onion, sliced
250 g (8 oz) tofu
2 tablespoons soy sauce
1 teaspoon finely chopped fresh root ginger
1 garlic clove, finely chopped
125 g (4 oz) cabbage, finely sliced
125 g (4 oz) bean sprouts
8 lychees, peeled, stoned and quartered
2 teaspoons blackstrap molasses

**To serve**
nori flakes
sesame seeds
lime wedges (optional)

Serves **2**
Prep time **10 minutes**
Cooking time **10 minutes**

# BALANCING ACT

A vegan diet can be healthy, nutritious and satisfying but it also requires a little extra thought and effort - especially when you're shopping for, and preparing, all your own meals. As you won't be getting quick-fix protein hits from ingredients such as meat, eggs and fish, and a daily calcium boost from dairy, you need to boost your intake from other sources. Student life can be hectic and vegans need to take extra care to ensure they're eating a balanced diet.

## STOCK UP ON SNACKS
Keep a handy supply of dried fruit, nuts and seeds in your cupboard so there's always something nutritious to munch on, whatever your time constraints. A good stock of ziplock food bags and small plastic boxes will make it easy to snack on the go.

## FRUIT AND VEG
Forget five a day, the advice now is to try and get your daily consumption of fresh fruit and veg closer to ten portions. Vegans are usually pretty good at including these in their diet but remember to choose a selection of different colours when you're shopping, as this will maximize the number of vitamins and nutrients in your daily diet.

### CARB-LOAD AT MEALTIMES
Rice, pasta and potatoes are prime sources of carbohydrates so try to include a hearty portion with each meal. This will give you energy and keep you full between meals.

### DAIRY ALTERNATIVES
Include soya, rice and other dairy alternatives in your meals and snacks to make sure you get enough calcium in your diet. Tofu is another good source so add this to your shopping list, too.

### PUMPING IRON
Aim for dark green on the vegetable colour chart. Broccoli, leafy vegetables and watercress are all good ways to maximize your iron intake. And don't wash the good stuff away by boiling your veg: always steam it to keep the vitamins intact.

### OMEGA-3
The main sources of omega-3 are oily fish, so you'll need to get your omega-3 fatty acids from other ingredients. Luckily, soya, nuts and rapeseed oil are all vegan-friendly and high in omega-3s.

### KEEP HYDRATED
Water has a vital part to play in helping you stay alert, focussed and full of energy, as well as helping to rid your body of unwanted nasties. Keep a bottle in your bag, a full glass on your desk and down a glass of water every time you're waiting for the kettle to boil.

# Malaysian COCONUT & VEGETABLE STEW

2 tablespoons vegetable oil
1 medium onion, thinly sliced
6 tablespoons laksa curry paste
2 × 400 ml (14 fl oz) cans coconut
  milk
1 teaspoon salt
300 ml (½ pint) water
200 g (7 oz) peeled potatoes, cut
  into 1.5 cm (¾ inch) pieces
250 g (8 oz) peeled carrots, cut
  into 1.5 cm (¾ inch) pieces
100 g (3½ oz) fine green beans,
  topped, tailed and halved
150 g (5 oz) cauliflower florets
300 g (10 oz) peeled and deseeded
  butternut squash, cut into 1.5 cm
  (¾ inch) pieces
50 g (2 oz) cashew nuts
50 g (2 oz) bean sprouts
4 spring onions, trimmed and
  sliced on the diagonal
handful of Thai sweet basil leaves
  or fresh coriander

Serves **4**
Prep time **5 minutes**
Cooking time **25 minutes**

1 Heat the oil in a large saucepan over a medium heat. Add the onion and the curry paste and fry gently for 2–3 minutes until it begins to smell fragrant.

2 Add the coconut milk, salt and measured water and bring to the boil.

3 Add the potatoes and carrots and cook for 10 minutes, then add the green beans, cauliflower and squash and cook for a further 7 minutes.

4 Add the cashew nuts and simmer for 3 minutes until the vegetables are just tender.

5 Stir in the bean sprouts, spring onions and basil or coriander. Simmer for 1 minute and serve immediately.

# THAI GREEN
## *Vegetable Curry*

1. Peel and slice the hard vegetables and cut into 2.5 cm (1 inch) cubes. Quarter the aubergines and slice the courgettes and mushrooms. Cut the asparagus into 2.5 cm (1 inch) pieces and top and tail the beans. Cook the hard vegetables in boiling water over a medium heat for 8-10 minutes, or until soft, then drain.

2. Heat the oil in a wok or saucepan. Stir-fry the curry paste and goji berries, if using, over a medium heat for 3-4 minutes until fragrant. Add the aubergines, courgettes and mushrooms and stir-fry for 4-5 minutes. Add the asparagus, sweetcorn and green beans and gently stir-fry for another 2-3 minutes.

3. Add the soya milk, soy sauce, sugar, cooked hard vegetables and pineapple and warm through for 2-3 minutes, stirring occasionally. Taste and adjust the seasoning.

4. Spoon into 4 serving bowls and garnish with Thai sweet basil leaves and chilli slices.

200 g (7 oz) mixed hard vegetables (such as pumpkin, winter squash and marrow)
225 g (8 oz) mixed soft vegetables (such as Thai aubergines, baby sweetcorn, courgettes, mushrooms, asparagus and green beans)
1½-2 tablespoons sunflower oil
2-3 tablespoons Thai green curry paste
25 sun-dried goji berries (optional)
475 ml (16 fl oz) soya milk
3 tablespoons light soy sauce
15 g (½ oz) coconut, palm or brown sugar
150 g (5 oz) pineapple or pineapple slices in light juice, cut into pieces

**To garnish**
Thai sweet basil, leaves picked
few slices of red chilli

Serves **4**
Prep time **15 minutes**
Cooking time **25 minutes**

## STUDENT TIP

**WEEKLY SHOP** Although it's tempting to top up your weekly groceries by popping into the convenience store on the way home from college, you'll pay more for the privilege. Instead, do a well-planned supermarket shop once a week for cheaper prices and bulk-buy deals.

AFFORDABILITY
2

# CHICKPEA & SPINACH CURRY

1. Place the chickpeas in a deep bowl and cover with cold water. Leave to soak overnight.

2. Transfer to a colander and rinse under cold running water. Drain and place in a saucepan. Cover with water and bring to the boil, then reduce the heat to low. Simmer gently for 45 minutes, skimming off any scum that rises to the surface and stirring often. Drain and set aside.

3. Meanwhile, heat the oil in a wok, add the onions and cook over a low heat for 15 minutes until lightly golden. Add the coriander, cumin, chilli powder, turmeric and curry powder and stir-fry for 1-2 minutes. Add the tomatoes, sugar and the measured water and bring to the boil. Cover, reduce the heat and simmer gently for 15 minutes.

4. Add the chickpeas, season to taste and cook gently for 8-10 minutes. Stir in the mint. Divide the spinach leaves between 4 shallow bowls and top with the chickpea mixture. Serve immediately with steamed rice or bread.

200 g (7 oz) dried chickpeas
1 tablespoon groundnut oil
2 onions, thinly sliced
2 teaspoons ground coriander
2 teaspoons ground cumin
1 teaspoon hot chilli powder
½ teaspoon ground turmeric
1 tablespoon medium curry powder
400 g (14 oz) can chopped tomatoes
1 teaspoon soft brown sugar
100 ml (3½ fl oz) water
2 tablespoons chopped mint leaves
100 g (3½ oz) baby spinach
salt

Serves **4**
Prep time **20 minutes, plus soaking**
Cooking time **1 hour**

AFFORDABILITY
1

# BLACK LENTIL *Curry*

1 Place the lentils in a deep bowl and cover with cold water. Leave to soak for 10-12 hours. Transfer to a colander and rinse under cold running water. Drain and place in a saucepan with half the measured water. Bring to the boil, reduce the heat to low and simmer for 35-40 minutes until tender. Drain and set aside.

2 Heat the oil in a large saucepan over a medium heat. Add the onion, garlic, ginger, chilli, cumin seeds and ground coriander, and stir-fry for 5-6 minutes until the onion is soft and translucent. Add the turmeric, paprika, kidney beans and cooked lentils, and stir thoroughly.

3 Add the remaining measured water and bring back to the boil. Reduce the heat to low and simmer gently for 10-15 minutes, stirring often. Remove from the heat and season to taste. Stir in the coriander and sprinkle over a little extra paprika. Serve immediately with the yogurt.

125 g (4 oz) dried whole black lentils, rinsed and drained
1 litre (1¾ pints) water
1 tablespoon groundnut oil
1 onion, finely chopped
3 garlic cloves, crushed
2 teaspoons peeled and finely grated fresh root ginger
1 fresh green chilli, halved lengthways
2 teaspoons cumin seeds
1 teaspoon ground coriander
1 teaspoon ground turmeric
1 teaspoon paprika, plus extra for sprinkling
200 g (7 oz) canned red kidney beans, rinsed and drained
large handful of chopped coriander leaves
salt
200 ml (7 fl oz) soya yogurt, whisked, to serve

Serves **4**
Prep time **20 minutes, plus soaking**
Cooking time **about 1 hour**

AFFORDABILITY 2

# Okra, Pea & Tomato
# CURRY

1 tablespoon groundnut oil
6–8 curry leaves
2 teaspoons black mustard seeds
1 onion, finely diced
2 teaspoons ground cumin
1 teaspoon ground coriander
2 teaspoons curry powder
1 teaspoon ground turmeric
3 garlic cloves, finely chopped
500 g (1 lb 2 oz) okra, cut on the
   diagonal into 2.5 cm (1 inch)
   pieces
200 g (7 oz) fresh or frozen peas
2 ripe plum tomatoes, finely
   chopped
salt and pepper
3 tablespoons grated fresh
   coconut, to serve

Serves **4**
Prep time **5 minutes**
Cooking time **about 20 minutes**

**1** Heat the oil in a large nonstick wok or frying pan over a medium heat. Add the curry leaves, mustard seeds and onion. Stir-fry for 3–4 minutes until fragrant and the onion is starting to soften, then add the cumin, coriander, curry powder and turmeric. Stir-fry for a further 1–2 minutes until fragrant.

**2** Add the garlic and okra, and increase the heat to high. Cook, stirring, for 2–3 minutes, then add the peas and tomatoes. Season to taste, cover and reduce the heat to low. Cook gently for 10–12 minutes, stirring occasionally, until the okra is just tender. Remove from the heat and sprinkle over the grated coconut just before serving.

**VARIATION**
For spiced seeded pea & tomato pilaf, place 300 g (10 oz) basmati rice in a medium saucepan with 2 teaspoons of dry-roasted cumin seeds, 1 tablespoon of crushed dry-roasted coriander seeds, 2 teaspoons of black mustard seeds, 200 g (7 oz) fresh or frozen peas and 3 peeled, deseeded and finely chopped tomatoes. Add 650 ml (1 pint 2 fl oz) boiling vegetable stock, bring to the boil and season to taste. Reduce the heat to low, cover the pan and cook gently for 10–12 minutes, or until all the liquid has been absorbed. Remove from the heat and allow to stand, covered and undisturbed, for 10–15 minutes. Fluff up the grains with a fork and serve.

# WILD RICE, PARSNIP & PEANUT Curry

AFFORDABILITY **2**

125 g (4 oz) wild rice, rinsed
3 tablespoons vegetable oil
2 onions, thinly sliced
3 garlic cloves, finely chopped
1 tablespoon vegan bouillon powder
1 tablespoon vegan hot curry paste
1 teaspoon ground turmeric
800 ml (1⅓ pints) boiling water
500 g (1 lb 2 oz) parsnips, cut into small chunks
100 g (3½ oz) tenderstem broccoli, stalks cut into 1 cm (½ inch) lengths
50 g (2 oz) crunchy peanut butter
3 tablespoons chopped coriander
50 g (2 oz) salted peanuts, roughly chopped
salt and pepper

Serves **4**
Prep time **15 minutes**
Cooking time **55 minutes**

1 Cook the wild rice in plenty of boiling water for about 30 minutes, or until the grains have softened but have not lost their shape. Drain.

2 Meanwhile, heat the oil in a large saucepan and gently fry the onions for 10 minutes until softened and golden. Stir in the garlic and cook for a further 1 minute. Add the bouillon powder, curry paste and turmeric and stir in the measured boiling water. Add the parsnips and bring to a gentle simmer. Cover with a lid and cook for 20 minutes.

3 Add the rice and broccoli and cook for a further 20 minutes until the rice and vegetables are very tender.

4 Ladle a little of the stock into a heatproof bowl or mug and stir in the peanut butter until softened in the stock. Tip into the curry and stir well until heated through. Season to taste with salt and pepper and ladle into bowls. Serve sprinkled with the coriander and peanuts.

# SPICY GOAN AUBERGINE CURRY

1 Dry-roast the cumin and coriander seeds in a nonstick frying pan over a low heat for 2–3 minutes until fragrant.

2 Remove from the heat and crush them lightly. Place them in a large saucepan with the chillies, turmeric, cayenne, garlic, ginger and the measured warm water.

3 Bring to the boil, reduce the heat and simmer for 10 minutes until thickened. Season to taste. Stir in the coconut milk and tamarind paste.

4 Arrange the aubergine slices in a foil-lined grill pan and brush with some of the curry sauce. Cook under a preheated hot grill, turning once, until golden and tender. Add the aubergine slices to the curry, gently heat and serve with naan bread or chapatis.

**VARIATION**
For cashew & courgette curry, add 200 g (7 oz) roasted cashew nuts to the finished curry sauce. To roast, soak in water for 20 minutes, then heat in a dry frying pan, shaking regularly, until lightly browned before chopping them. Replace the aubergine with 4 sliced courgettes and grill as above. Drizzle with walnut oil and season to taste before adding to the curry sauce.

1 teaspoon cumin seeds
4 teaspoons coriander seeds
2 fresh green chillies, deseeded and sliced
½ teaspoon ground turmeric
1 teaspoon cayenne pepper
4 garlic cloves, crushed
1 tablespoon peeled and grated fresh root ginger
300 ml (½ pint) warm water
400 ml (14 fl oz) reduced-fat coconut milk
1 tablespoon tamarind paste
1 large aubergine, thinly sliced lengthways
salt and pepper

Serves **4**
Prep time **15 minutes**
Cooking time **25 minutes**

AFFORDABILITY
2

# MILD COCONUT CURRY

1 Put the potatoes, lemon grass and lentils into a medium saucepan and add enough boiling water to just cover the tops of the potatoes. Return to the boil, then simmer for about 15 minutes.

2 Heat the oil in a large saucepan and fry the onion, garlic, mushrooms, turmeric and cumin until the onion is soft. Add all the remaining ingredients, except for the coriander, and stir well.

3 Remove the lemon grass from the lentil pan, then add the lentils and potatoes to the onion mixture.

4 Simmer everything for about 10 minutes, or until the lentils are soft, then add the chopped coriander.

5 Serve with brown basmati rice cooked with a few cardamom pods, plus warm naan bread made without milk or yogurt.

2 medium potatoes, chopped
1 lemon grass stalk
4 tablespoons Puy lentils
1 tablespoon coconut oil
1 onion, chopped
2 garlic cloves, chopped
6 mushrooms, sliced
1 teaspoon ground turmeric
1 teaspoon ground cumin
125 g (4 oz) green beans
1 yellow pepper, cored, deseeded and chopped
1 courgette, chopped
250 g (8 oz) frozen sweetcorn
300 ml (½ pint) can coconut milk
juice of 1 lime
1 tablespoon chopped coriander leaves

Serves **4**
Prep time **15 minutes**
Cooking time **30 minutes**

AFFORDABILITY 2

# Jamaican-style
## BEAN, COURGETTE & COCONUT

**AFFORDABILITY 1**

1 Heat the coconut oil in a large saucepan and gently fry the onions for 5 minutes, stirring frequently. Add the courgettes and fry for a further 8–10 minutes until deep golden. Stir in the ginger, dried chillies, coriander seeds, mustard seeds, cayenne pepper and turmeric and fry, stirring continuously, for 2 minutes. Add the garlic and fry for a further 1 minute.

2 Tip in the black-eyed beans, coconut cream, stock and sugar and bring to a gentle simmer. Cover with a lid and cook for 5 minutes.

3 Add the potatoes and continue to cook for a further 25–30 minutes until all the vegetables are completely tender and the juices are thickened. Serve in bowls with lime wedges for drizzling.

3 tablespoons coconut oil
2 onions, chopped
500 g (1 lb 2 oz) courgettes, cut into 1 cm (½ inch) chunks
20 g (¾ oz) piece of fresh root ginger, finely chopped
¼ teaspoon crushed dried chillies
2 teaspoons coriander seeds, lightly crushed
1 tablespoon black or yellow mustard seeds
½ teaspoon cayenne pepper
1 teaspoon ground turmeric
2 garlic cloves, finely chopped
400 g (14 oz) can black-eyed beans, drained and rinsed
150 ml (¼ pint) coconut cream
300 ml (½ pint) vegetable stock (see page 219)
1 teaspoon light muscovado sugar
500 g (1 lb 2 oz) baking potatoes, cut into 2 cm (¾ inch) chunks
lime wedges, to serve

Serves **4**
Prep time **20 minutes**
Cooking time **55 minutes**

## STUDENT TIP

**BEFRIEND YOUR FREEZER** Whether it's freezing leftovers or making and freezing extra portions, you'll save time and money by stocking up on some future meals. Always label bags and containers or dinner will be a lucky dip.

# CAULIFLOWER & CHICKPEA
# Pan-fry

6 tablespoons olive oil
1 red onion, cut into thin wedges
½ cauliflower, cut into small florets
1 teaspoon garam masala
1 teaspoon ground coriander
28 chard leaves, washed, patted
   dry and cut into strips
1 teaspoon cumin seeds
1 garlic clove, thinly sliced
400 g (14 oz) can chickpeas,
   drained and rinsed
5 tablespoons tahini
4 tablespoons lemon juice
4 tablespoons water, plus 150 ml
   (¼ pint) water
salt and pepper
vegan naan bread, to serve

Serves **4**
Prep time **20 minutes**
Cooking time **20 minutes**

**1** Heat the oil in a large, heavy-based frying pan or wok, add the onion and cook over a medium-high heat, stirring frequently, for 3-4 minutes until beginning to soften.

**2** Add the cauliflower florets, the garam masala and coriander and cook for 5 minutes, stirring almost constantly to prevent the cauliflower from catching, then add the 4 tablespoons of cold water. Cook for a further 2 minutes and keep stirring.

**3** Stir the chard, cumin and garlic into the pan and cook, stirring, for a further 2 minutes. Add the chickpeas along with the tahini, lemon juice and the remaining 150 ml (¼ pint) water and season with salt and pepper. Toss the vegetables in the sauce, then reduce the heat, cover and simmer for 2 minutes. Season generously with salt and pepper.

**4** Toss again before serving in warmed serving bowls with naan bread.

**VARIATION**
For curried broccoli pan-fry with cumin seeds, heat 3 tablespoons of olive oil in a large, heavy-based frying pan or wok, add 1 large white onion, thinly sliced into wedges, and stir-fry over a medium-high heat for 2 minutes. Add 300 g (10 oz) small broccoli florets and 1 red pepper, cored, deseeded and thinly sliced, and stir-fry for 3-4 minutes until softened. Add 2 tablespoons of curry paste and 1 teaspoon of cumin seeds and cook, stirring, for a further 1 minute. Add 2 tablespoons of mango chutney, season with salt and pepper if necessary and toss again for 1 minute. Serve piled on to 2 warmed, halved naan breads.

# TAKEOUT
# ALTERNATIVES

The weekly takeaway treat can prove tricky for vegans: many options are completely off limits, while those that sound safe can't always be properly checked, as menus don't list the full ingredients. But don't let that put you off enjoying the same types of takeaway dishes as your housemates. It's quick, easy – and a whole lot cheaper – to make your own takeout meals at home. Here are a few ideas to get you started.

### INDIAN
Tarka dahl is simple to make and a big batch can be split into individual portions. Serve with poppadoms (naturally dairy free) or naan bread (check it's dairy free, milk is often used in the ingredients). Another spicy vegan-friendly Indian dish is chana masala, made with spices and chickpeas. Sag aloo (spinach and potatoes), many rice dishes and some baltis and biryanis are vegan, too.

### CHINESE

When it comes to making your own Chinese takeaway at home, tofu is your friend. So many Chinese dishes feature this tasty ingredient, simply cubed, fried and cooked in sauce. Add a handful of cashew nuts for extra texture. Steamed Chinese greens with seeds, stir-fried rice with peas, and vegetarian noodles will turn the meal into a banquet.

### BURGER AND FRIES

Dairy-free buns are easy to source these days and the meat-free options for fillings are endless: lightly grill large mushrooms, peppers and soya meat alternatives and add vegan cheese, or thick slices of beef tomatoes. And when it comes to chips – choose French fries, skin-on chips or wedges with plenty of dipping sauce and salt. Serve on paper plates or wrapped in greaseproof paper for extra authenticity.

### PIZZA

There's a fairly good selection of vegan pizzas now available in supermarkets but it's easy to make your own batch of pizza dough and top it with non-dairy cheese, tomatoes and other ingredients such as olives, capers, peppers and sweetcorn. So, there's no need to miss out on this student favourite!

### KEBAB

This popular post-pub snack needn't be off limits to vegans – but you might have to wait until you get home to enjoy it. Turkish bread, naan bread or pitta all work well and can be stuffed with a soya meat alternative, shredded iceberg, salsa or chilli sauce.

# BLACK-EYED BEAN &
## RED PEPPER 'STEW'

2 tablespoons olive oil
4 shallots, finely chopped
2 garlic cloves, crushed
2 celery stalks, diced
1 large carrot, peeled and cut into
1 cm (½ inch) pieces
1 red pepper, cored, deseeded and
cut into 1 cm (½ inch) pieces
1 teaspoon dried mixed herbs
2 teaspoons ground cumin
1 teaspoon ground cinnamon
2 × 400 g (14 oz) cans chopped
tomatoes
2 tablespoons sun-dried tomato
purée
75 ml (3 fl oz) vegetable stock
(see page 219)
2 × 400 g (14 oz) cans black-eyed
beans in water, drained and
rinsed
4 tablespoons finely chopped
coriander leaves, plus extra
to garnish
salt and pepper
cooked basmati rice, to serve

Serves **4**
Prep time **10 minutes**
Cooking time **20 minutes**

1 Heat the oil in a large frying pan and place over a high heat. Add the shallots, garlic, celery, carrot and red pepper and stir-fry for 2-3 minutes, or until lightly starting to brown.

2 Add the dried herbs, cumin, cinnamon, tomatoes, tomato purée and stock and bring to the boil. Reduce the heat to medium, cover and cook gently for 12-15 minutes, or until the vegetables are tender, breaking up the tomatoes into small pieces with a wooden spoon towards the end of the cooking time.

3 Stir in the black-eyed beans and cook for 2-3 minutes, or until piping hot.

4 Season well, remove from the heat and sprinkle over the chopped coriander. Garnish with coriander leaves and serve with basmati rice.

# PEPPER & LENTIL STEW
## with Cornbread Muffins

1  Cook the lentils in boiling water for 20 minutes to soften. In a separate pan, melt the coconut oil and fry the peppers and onion for about 12 minutes or until pale golden, stirring frequently. Add the garlic and fry for a further 1 minute.

2  Stir in the Cajun spice, coconut milk, stock and tomato purée. Drain the lentils, add to the pan and bring to a simmer. Cook gently for 15 minutes.

3  For the muffins, line six sections of a muffin tin with paper muffin cases. Put the flour, cornmeal or polenta, baking powder, chilli flakes, cheese, half the coriander and a little salt in a bowl and mix well.

4  In a small saucepan melt the dairy-free spread over a low heat and combine with the milk. Add the milk mixture to the bowl and stir with a round bladed knife until the ingredients are just combined. Divide among the paper muffin cases.

5  Bake in a preheated oven, 220°C (425°F), Gas Mark 7 for 20 minutes until risen and just beginning to colour. Stir the remaining coriander into the peppers and lentils, heat through gently and spoon into bowls. Serve with the muffins.

200 g (7 oz) Puy lentils, rinsed
2 tablespoons coconut oil
1 red pepper, cored, deseeded and cut into chunks
1 orange pepper, cored, deseeded and cut into chunks
1 green pepper, cored, deseeded and cut into chunks
2 onions, chopped
2 garlic cloves, crushed
1 tablespoon Cajun spice mix
400ml (14fl oz) can coconut milk
250ml (7½ fl oz) vegetable stock (see page 219)
3 tablespoons tomato purée

**Muffins**
125 g (4 oz) self-raising flour
125 g (4 oz) cornmeal or polenta
1 teaspoon baking powder
½ teaspoon dried chilli flakes
75 g (3 oz) Cheddar-style vegan cheese, grated
20 g (¾ oz) coriander, chopped
3 tablespoons dairy-free spread
150 ml (¼ pint) rice or oat milk
salt

Serves **6**
Prep time **25 minutes**
Cooking time **1 hour**

AFFORDABILITY

# QUICK VEGETABLE MOLE

1 Heat the oil in a large saucepan, add the onion and garlic and cook over a medium heat for 2-3 minutes until softened. Add the sweet potatoes and red pepper and cook for 2 minutes.

2 Stir in the chilli powder, tomatoes, stock and all the beans and bring to the boil. Reduce the heat, cover and simmer gently for 20-25 minutes until the vegetables are tender. Season to taste with salt and pepper.

3 Add the chocolate and coriander and cook for a further 2-3 minutes. Serve with long-grain rice topped with spoonfuls of natural soya yogurt, if liked.

## VARIATION

For Mexican bean soup, heat 1 tablespoon of sunflower oil in a frying pan, add 1 chopped onion, 1 chopped celery stick, 2 diced carrots and 1 cored, deseeded and chopped red pepper and cook over a medium heat for 5-6 minutes until softened. Stir in 1 tablespoon of chilli powder, 400 g (14 oz) can chopped tomatoes, a 400 g (14 oz) can each of red kidney beans and black beans, drained and rinsed, and 600 ml (1 pint) hot vegetable stock. Simmer for 10 minutes. Stir in 15 g (½ oz) grated plain dark dairy-free chocolate and serve in bowls, garnished with chopped spring onions, chopped fresh coriander and a spoonful of natural soya yogurt, if liked.

1 tablespoon sunflower oil
1 large onion, chopped
1 garlic clove, crushed
400 g (14 oz) sweet potatoes, peeled and cut into small chunks
1 large red pepper, cored, deseeded and chopped
1 tablespoon chilli powder
2 × 400 g (14 oz) cans chopped tomatoes
150 ml (¼ pint) vegetable stock (see page 219)
400 g (14 oz) can red kidney beans, drained and rinsed
400 g (14 oz) can black beans, drained and rinsed
15 g (½ oz) dairy-free plain dark chocolate, grated
2 tablespoons chopped fresh coriander
salt and black pepper

Serves **4**
Prep time **10 minutes**
Cooking time **30-35 minutes**

AFFORDABILITY
1

# SPINACH & MUSHROOM
## *Lasagne*

1 Melt 1 tablespoon of the dairy-free spread in a large frying pan or wide-based saucepan and fry the onions and celery for 5 minutes. Add the mushrooms and fry for a further 10 minutes until the mushrooms are lightly browned and all the liquid has evaporated.

2 Stir in the garlic, herbs, and red wine and cook for a couple of minutes. Stir in the tomato paste. Gradually add the spinach, turning it in the hot sauce until wilted. Season to taste with salt and pepper.

3 Melt the remaining dairy-free spread in a saucepan, add the flour and cook for 1 minute. Gradually blend in the milk, stirring well to remove any lumps. Cook for 3-4 minutes until thickened. Stir in the nutritional yeast, if using, or season with salt and pepper.

4 To assemble, spoon a quarter of the mushroom sauce in a shallow ovenproof dish and spread level. Arrange a single layer of lasagne sheets on top, snapping the sheets to fit where necessary. Drizzle with about a third of the white sauce. Spoon another quarter of the mushroom sauce into the dish and arrange more lasagne sheets on top.

5 Repeat with another layer of mushroom sauce and lasagne sheets then spread with the remaining mushroom sauce. Spoon the rest of the white sauce on top and sprinkle with the cheese.

6 Bake in a preheated oven, 180°C (350°F), Gas Mark 4, for 50-60 minutes until the surface is bubbling and golden. Leave to stand for 10 minutes before serving.

4 tablespoons dairy-free spread
2 onions, chopped
2 sticks celery, chopped
625 g (1¼ lb) mushrooms, roughly chopped
3 garlic cloves, crushed
2 teaspoons dried thyme or oregano
150 ml (¼ pint) vegan red wine
3 tablespoons sun-dried tomato purée
450 g (1 lb) spinach, washed and dried
4 tablespoons plain flour
600 ml (1 pint) almond milk
3 tablespoons nutritional yeast (optional)
200 g (7 oz) lasagne sheets
100 g (3½ oz) Cheddar-style vegan cheese, grated
salt and pepper

Serves **4-5**
Prep time **35 minutes**
Cooking time **1 hour 20 minutes**

AFFORDABILITY
2

# VEGAN *Moussaka*

2 medium aubergines, cut into
  5 mm (¼ inch) thick slices
4 tablespoons olive oil
500 g (1 lb 2 oz) Charlotte or
  Jersey Royal potatoes, scrubbed
  and cut into 5 mm (¼ inch)
  slices
2 red onions, chopped
4 garlic cloves, crushed
150 ml (¼ pint) vegan red wine
200 g (7 oz) plain, olive or basil
  tofu
1 teaspoon dried oregano or
  thyme
1 teaspoon ground cinnamon
2 tablespoons tomato purée
2 tablespoons dairy-free spread
3 tablespoons plain flour
450 ml (¾ pint) almond milk
3 tablespoons nutritional yeast
  (optional)
salt and pepper

Serves **4**
Prep time **10 minutes**
Cooking time **1 hour**

AFFORDABILITY
**3**

1  Place the aubergine slices on a foil-lined grill rack or baking sheet and brush with 2 tablespoons of the oil. Season with salt and pepper and cook under a moderate grill for 10 minutes until golden. Turn the slices over and cook for a further 10 minutes.

2  Meanwhile, cook the potatoes in boiling, lightly salted water for 5 minutes, and drain.

3  Heat the remaining oil in a frying pan and fry the onions for 5 minutes to soften. Add the garlic and cook for a further 1 minute. Add the wine and let it bubble for a couple of minutes. Crumble in the tofu then add the oregano or thyme, cinnamon and tomato purée. Cook for 2 minutes, stirring to combine the ingredients.

4  Melt the dairy-free spread in the rinsed-out saucepan, add the flour and cook for 1 minute. Gradually blend in the milk, stirring well to remove any lumps. Cook for 1-2 minutes until thickened. Stir in the nutritional yeast, if using, or season with salt and pepper.

5  To assemble, spread half the tofu mixture in a shallow ovenproof dish and arrange half the potatoes and aubergine slices on top. Spoon about a third of the sauce on top. Add the remaining tofu mixture, potatoes and finally the aubergines. Spread with the rest of the sauce. Bake in a preheated oven, 190°C (375°F), Gas Mark 5, for 45 minutes. Serve with a leafy salad.

# SWEET POTATO, PEPPER & COCONUT Gratin

1 Combine the peppers, onion, garlic and chilli and scatter about two-thirds over the base of a shallow baking dish.

2 Place the potato slices vertically into the dish over the pepper mixture. Once all the slices are packed into the dish, scatter the remaining pepper mixture around the potatoes.

3 Put the peanut butter and coconut milk in a small saucepan and heat gently until the peanut butter softens enough to combine smoothly with the coconut milk. Pour over the potatoes and cover the dish with foil.

4 Bake in a preheated oven, 190°C (375°F), Gas Mark 5, for 30 minutes. Uncover the dish and bake for a further 50-60 minutes until the potatoes are very soft when pierced with a knife and the surface is turning golden.

2 romano red peppers, cored, deseeded and finely chopped
1 red onion, finely chopped
3 garlic cloves, finely chopped
1 red chilli, deseeded and finely chopped
1 kg (2 lb) medium-sized sweet potatoes, scrubbed and thinly sliced
75 g (3 oz) crunchy peanut butter
400 ml (14 fl oz) can coconut milk

Serves **4**
Prep time **25 minutes**
Cooking time **1½ hours**

# MUSHROOM STROGANOFF

5 tablespoons olive oil
450 g (1 lb) mixed mushrooms, such as chestnut, chanterelle, shiitake and button, trimmed and halved or quartered if large
1 garlic clove, thinly sliced
1 large red onion, halved and thinly sliced
2 tablespoons brandy
1 teaspoon wholegrain mustard
½ teaspoon English mustard
½ teaspoon ground paprika
2 tablespoons cashew butter
250 ml (9 fl oz) soya cream
4 tablespoons chopped flat leaf parsley
salt and pepper

Serves **4**
Prep time **15 minutes**
Cooking time **10 minutes**

**1** Heat the oil in a large, heavy-based frying pan, add the mushrooms, garlic and onion and cook over a high heat, stirring occasionally, for 5 minutes until golden and softened.

**2** Add the brandy, mustards and paprika and continue to cook, stirring and tossing constantly, for 1–2 minutes.

**3** Stir in the cashew butter and soya cream and gently heat for 1 minute until piping hot but not boiling, otherwise the cream may separate.

**4** Stir in the chopped parsley and season with a little salt and plenty of pepper. Serve on a bed of rice.

**VARIATION**
For vegetable stroganoff, heat 3 tablespoons of olive oil in a large, heavy-based frying pan, add 1 large onion, thinly sliced, 2 sweet potatoes, peeled and cubed, and 1 red pepper, cored, deseeded and cubed, and cook over a medium heat, stirring occasionally, for 5 minutes until the onion is softened but not browned. Add 6 tablespoons of water and stir again. Cover and simmer very gently for 5 minutes, or until the sweet potato is tender. Add ½ teaspoon of ground paprika and toss again, then stir in 200 ml (7 fl oz) cashew cream and 4 tablespoons of chopped flat leaf parsley and heat for 1–2 minutes over a gentle heat until piping hot but not boiling, otherwise the cream may separate. Season well with salt and pepper and serve on a bed of rice.

# ROSTI TART
## WITH AUBERGINES & RED ONIONS

750 g (1½ lb) waxy potatoes
4 tablespoons olive oil
2 teaspoons finely chopped
  rosemary
3 red onions, sliced
1 large aubergine, cut into 2 cm
  (¾ inch) dice
2 garlic cloves, crushed
150 g (5 oz) pizza-style vegan
  cheese, grated
12 pitted black olives
3 tablespoons capers
salt and pepper

Serves **4-6**
Prep time **30 minutes**
Cooking time **40 minutes**

**1** Line a 35 × 25 cm (14 × 10 inch) Swiss roll tin or similar sized baking tray with a rectangle of baking paper that comes up the sides.

**2** Coarsely grate the potatoes on to several layers of kitchen paper. Spread the potatoes in a thin layer and place more layers of kitchen paper on top. Press the paper down firmly to squeeze out the juice from the potatoes.

**3** Turn the potatoes into a bowl, add 2 tablespoons of the oil, the rosemary, plenty of pepper and a little salt. Turn into the tray and spread to the edges in an even layer. Pack down firmly with the back of a large spoon. Bake in a preheated oven, 200°C (400°F), Gas Mark 6, for 30 minutes or until golden and cooked through.

**4** While the potatoes are baking, heat the remaining oil in a frying pan and fry the onions and aubergine for 10 minutes, or until softened and golden. Stir in the garlic for a further 1 minute.

**5** Turn the vegetables out on to the potato base, spreading in an even layer. Sprinkle with the cheese and scatter with the olives and capers. Return to the oven for a further 10 minutes to melt the cheese.

**6** Cut into squares and transfer to serving plates with a fish slice. Serve with a rocket or watercress salad.

# TOMATO & THYME *Tart*

1. Put the flour in a bowl and season with salt and pepper. Add the spread and rub in with your fingertips until the mixture resembles fine breadcrumbs. Stir in half the thyme, then add enough of the measured water to bring the mixture together into a firm dough.

2. Roll the dough out on a lightly floured surface and use to line a 23 cm (9 inch) fluted flan tin. Chill until ready to use.

3. Heat 1 tablespoon of the oil in a frying pan, add the onion and cook over a medium-high heat for 5-6 minutes until softened and golden. Stir in the remaining thyme leaves and cook for a further 1 minute. Spoon the onion mixture into the pastry case and smooth over.

4. Toss the tomatoes in a bowl with the remaining oil, salt flakes and plenty of pepper. Arrange on top of the onion in the pastry case and bake in a preheated oven, 220°C (425°F), Gas Mark 7, for 20-25 minutes until the pastry is golden and the tomatoes softened and lightly charred in places. Garnish with thyme leaves to serve.

250 g (8 oz) plain flour, plus extra for dusting
125 g (4 oz) dairy-free spread, cubed
4 tablespoons thyme leaves, plus extra to garnish
2-3 tablespoons cold water
3 tablespoons olive oil
1 onion, finely chopped
250 g (8 oz) cherry tomatoes (in a mix of colours), halved
½ teaspoon sea salt flakes
salt and pepper

Serves **6**
Prep time **20 minutes, plus chilling**
Cooking time **35 minutes**

AFFORDABILITY 1

# CHICKPEA, CARROT & PRUNE *Pasties*

400 g (14 oz) can chickpeas
3 tablespoons olive oil
1 large onion, chopped
300 g (10 oz) carrots, diced
2 garlic cloves, crushed
2 teaspoons ras el hanout spice mix
1 teaspoon ground turmeric
100 g (3½ oz) pitted prunes, roughly chopped
3 tablespoons chopped coriander
salt and pepper

**Pastry**
325 g (11 oz) plain flour
175 g (6 oz) dairy-free spread, chilled
4 tablespoons water
oat or rice milk, to glaze
sea salt, to sprinkle

Makes **6**
Prep time **25 minutes, plus cooling**
Cooking time **50 minutes**

1 To make the pastry, put the flour in a bowl with a little salt and pepper. Add the dairy-free spread to the bowl, a little at a time, dusting with flour from the bowl each time so that the spread doesn't clump together. Once all the spread has been added to the flour, add the measured water and mix with a round-bladed knife until the mixture starts to form a dough. Add a dash more water if the mixture is still dry.

2 Turn out on to the surface and lightly knead into a ball of dough. Wrap and chill for at least 1 hour.

3 For the filling, drain the chickpeas, reserving the liquid. Break up the chickpeas by mashing them against the side of the bowl with a fork. Heat the oil in a frying pan and fry the onion and carrots for 10 minutes, stirring frequently. Add the garlic, spice mix and turmeric and fry for another 1 minute. Remove from the heat and stir in the chickpeas, chickpea liquid, prunes and coriander. Season to taste with salt and pepper.

4 Line a large baking sheet with baking paper. Divide the pastry into 6 even-sized pieces and roll out each on a floured surface to a circle measuring about 18 cm (7 inches) in diameter. Spoon the filling on to the pastry pieces, slightly to one side of the centre. Fold the pastry over to enclose the filling and press the edges firmly together to seal. Press and crimp the edges of the pastry to seal, and transfer to the baking sheet. Brush with milk and sprinkle with sea salt.

5 Bake for about 40 minutes in a preheated oven, 200°C (400°F), Gas Mark 6, until the pastry is firm and just beginning to brown. Serve warm or cold.

# Chestnut COTTAGE PIES

1 Cover the dried chestnuts with the stock and soak overnight, or boil them in the stock for 1 hour.

2 Place both types of potatoes into a saucepan of water, bring to the boil, then simmer until soft, about 25 minutes.

3 Meanwhile, heat the olive oil in a pan and add the tomatoes, the remaining vegetables, dates, yeast extract and rosemary. Add the chestnuts and any remaining soaking liquid to this mixture and simmer for 15–20 minutes.

4 Drain the potatoes and mash them with the soya milk. Stir in the parsley, plus some salt and pepper.

5 Place the cornflour and carob in a small bowl, add the vinegar, molasses, tomato purée and orange juice and mix into a paste. Add the paste to the chestnut mixture, then stir over a low heat until the liquid thickens.

6 Divide the chestnut mixture equally between 6 individual pie dishes, each one 12 cm (5 inch). Place a layer of mashed potato on top. Bake in a preheated oven, 180°C (350°F), Gas Mark 4, for about 20 minutes until lightly browned.

125 g (4 oz) dried chestnuts
1.2 litres (2 pints) vegetable stock
  (see page 219)
750 g (1½ lb) potatoes, chopped
1 sweet potato, chopped
1 tablespoon olive oil
6 tomatoes, chopped
2 onions, chopped
1 carrot, chopped
125 g (4 oz) cauliflower, chopped
125 g (4 oz) frozen peas
1 green pepper, cored, deseeded
  and chopped
1 small courgette, chopped
1 tablespoon chopped dates
1 tablespoon yeast extract
6 sprigs of rosemary, leaves finely
  chopped
3 tablespoons sweetened soya
  milk
1 tablespoon chopped parsley
1 heaped tablespoon cornflour
1 teaspoon carob powder
1 tablespoon balsamic vinegar
1 teaspoon blackstrap molasses
2 teaspoons tomato purée
4 teaspoons orange juice
salt and pepper

Serves **6**
Prep time **20 minutes**
Cooking time **45 minutes, plus
  soaking**

AFFORDABILITY
3

# POTATO, ROSEMARY & ONION PIE

8 tablespoons olive oil

1 large Spanish onion, halved and thinly sliced

1 kg (2 lb) potatoes, scrubbed and thinly sliced

5 tablespoons chopped rosemary leaves

½ teaspoon dried chilli flakes

½ teaspoon ground cumin

½ teaspoon ground coriander

150 ml (¼ pint) vegetable stock (see page 219)

500 g (1 lb 2 oz) ready-made vegan puff pastry

plain flour, for dusting

2 tablespoons soya milk

salt and pepper

Serves **4**
Prep time **30 minutes**
Cooking time **about 45 minutes**

1   Heat half the oil in a frying pan, add the onion and cook over a medium-high heat for 5 minutes until softened and beginning to turn golden. Remove and set aside.

2   Heat the remaining oil in the pan, add the potato slices, rosemary and spices and cook, tossing and stirring frequently, for 10 minutes until softened and lightly golden.

3   Layer the potato slices in a large pie dish with the onions. Pour over the stock and season with salt and pepper.

4   Roll the pastry out on a lightly floured surface to about 1.5 cm (¾ inch) wider than the top of the pie dish. Cut a thin strip of pastry and place around the edge of the dish, pressing down with a little water to seal. Lightly brush the top of the strip with water, top with the pastry lid and press around the edges with a fork to seal. Make an incision in the centre of the pie for the steam to escape and lightly brush all over with the soya milk.

5   Bake in a preheated oven, 220°C (425°F), Gas Mark 7, for 25-30 minutes until the pastry is golden and the potatoes are tender. Serve hot.

AFFORDABILITY
1

# POTATO, MUSHROOM & ALE PIE

3 tablespoons vegetable oil
500 g (1 lb 2 oz) chestnut
  mushrooms, halved, or quartered
  if large
2 onions, thinly sliced
2 carrots, diced
3 garlic cloves, crushed
2 tablespoons plain flour
350 ml (12 fl oz) vegan ale
250 ml (8 fl oz) water
2 teaspoons vegan bouillon powder
2 teaspoons vegan Dijon mustard
1 teaspoon dried mixed herbs
500 g (1 lb 2 oz) baking potatoes,
  cut into small chunks

**Pastry**
200 g (7 oz) self-raising flour
125 g (4 oz) dairy-free spread, chilled
3 tablespoons water
oat or rice milk, to glaze
salt and pepper
sea salt, to sprinkle

Serves **4**
Prep time **30 minutes,
  plus chilling and cooling**
Cooking time **1 hour 10 minutes**

1 To make the pastry, put the flour in a bowl with a little salt and pepper. Add the dairy-free spread to the bowl, a little at a time, dusting with flour from the bowl each time so that the spread doesn't clump together. Once all the spread has been added, add the measured water and mix with a round-bladed knife until the mixture starts to form a dough. Turn out on to the surface and lightly knead into a ball of dough. Wrap and chill for at least 1 hour.

2 Heat 1 tablespoon of the oil in a large saucepan and gently fry the mushrooms, stirring them frequently for about 10 minutes until all the juices have evaporated and the mushrooms are browned. Tip out on to a plate.

3 Add the remaining oil to the pan with the onions and carrots and fry for a further 10 minutes. Stir in the garlic and flour and cook, stirring, for 1 minute. Gradually blend in the ale and the measured water.

4 Add the bouillon powder, mustard, herbs and potatoes and bring to a gentle simmer. Cook for about 10 minutes until the potatoes are beginning to soften. Turn into a pie dish, piling the vegetables up in the centre. Leave to cool.

5 Brush the edges of the pie dish with water. Roll out the pastry on a lightly floured surface and position over the pie. Neaten the edges and make a hole in the centre of the pie. Brush with the milk and sprinkle with sea salt. Bake in a preheated oven, 200°C (400°F), Gas Mark 6, for about 35-40 minutes until the pastry is golden. Serve hot with green vegetables.

# LENTIL, CAULIFLOWER & Potato PIE

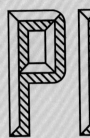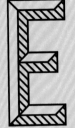

1. Melt 2 tablespoons of the dairy-free spread in a large saucepan and gently fry the onion, leek, carrots and celery for 5 minutes. Pour in the milk and bring to a gentle simmer. Add the lentils and bouillon powder, cover and cook gently for 30 minutes until the lentils are tender and the milk has thickened. Stir in the chestnuts and parsley and season to taste with salt and pepper. Transfer to a shallow pie dish.

2. Cook the potatoes in a large saucepan of boiling water for 8 minutes. Add the cauliflower and cook for a further 8–10 minutes, or until the vegetables are tender. Drain thoroughly, return to the pan and mash well.

3. Add the remaining dairy-free spread and mustard to the mash and season to taste with salt and pepper. Spoon over the filling and spread in an even layer. Bake in a preheated oven, 190°C (375°F), Gas Mark 5, for 40–50 minutes until crisped and pale golden. Serve with a seasonal green vegetable.

4 tablespoons dairy-free spread
1 onion, chopped
1 leek, trimmed and sliced
2 carrots, sliced
2 celery sticks, sliced
600 ml (1 pint) almond or oat milk
175 g (6 oz) Puy lentils, rinsed
1 tablespoon vegan bouillon powder
200 g (7 oz) cooked peeled chestnuts
10 g (⅓ oz) parsley, chopped
750 g (1½ lb) baking potatoes, cut into chunks
1 medium cauliflower, cut into chunks
2 tablespoons grainy mustard
salt and pepper

Serves **4**
Prep time **25 minutes**
Cooking time **1½ hours**

AFFORDABILITY 2

# RATATOUILLE PIE
## with parsnip mash

5 tablespoons olive oil
1 red pepper, cored, deseeded and cut into chunks
1 green pepper, cored, deseeded and cut into chunks
1 yellow pepper, cored, deseeded and cut into chunks
1 garlic clove, thinly sliced
1 large aubergine, trimmed and cut into chunks
2 courgettes, trimmed and cut into chunks
5 tomatoes, roughly chopped
150 ml (¼ pint) vegan red wine
150 ml (¼ pint) water
1 vegan stock cube
1.1 kg (2½ lb) parsnips, peeled and chopped
2 tablespoons soya spread
1 tablespoon chopped thyme leaves
salt and pepper

Serves **6**
Prep time **25 minutes**
Cooking time **45 minutes**

1 Heat the oil in a large, heavy-based frying pan, add the peppers, garlic, aubergine and courgettes and cook over a medium-high heat, stirring and tossing occasionally, for 10 minutes until softened and lightly golden in places. Add the tomatoes and cook for 3 minutes. Pour in the wine and measured water and bring to the boil, then cover and simmer for a further 10 minutes.

2 Meanwhile, bring a large saucepan of lightly salted water to the boil, crumble in the stock cube with the parsnips and mix well. Bring to a gentle simmer and cook for 10-15 minutes until the parsnips are tender. Drain well, return to the pan and mash with the soya spread, then stir in the thyme leaves.

3 Transfer the ratatouille mixture to a large gratin dish. Spoon the mashed parsnips over the vegetables and season generously with pepper. Bake in a preheated oven, 200°C (400°F), Gas Mark 6, for 20 minutes until the top is lightly golden in places. Serve with a simple green salad.

### VARIATION

For roasted vegetable & parsnip tray bake, cut 3 different-coloured peppers into chunks, then put in a large roasting tin along with 2 courgettes, trimmed and cut into chunks, and 2 parsnips, peeled and cut into chunks. Drizzle with 4 tablespoons of olive oil, sprinkle with 2 tablespoons of chopped rosemary and season with salt and pepper. Roast in a preheated oven, 200°C (400°F), Gas Mark 6, for 20 minutes until soft and lightly golden in places. Add 4 tomatoes, cut into chunks, to the tin and gently toss, then roast for a further 10 minutes. Serve hot in warmed serving bowls with crusty bread to mop up the juices.

# POTATO & PEPPER SALTADO

1 Cook the potatoes in boiling, lightly salted water for about 3 minutes until slightly softened but keeping their shape. Drain thoroughly in a sieve and pat dry between several sheets of kitchen paper.

2 Put the cornflour in a small bowl and gradually blend in the measured water. Add the coriander, dried herbs, soy sauce, vinegar, mustard and sugar. Mix well.

3 Heat 2 tablespoons of the oil in a frying pan and tip in the potatoes. Cook gently for about 10 minutes, turning the potatoes frequently until golden brown and cooked through. Drain the potatoes to a plate. Tip the nuts into the pan and cook briefly until lightly browned. Add to the plate with the potatoes.

4 Add the remaining oil to the frying pan with the peppers and onions and fry gently for 10-12 minutes until both onion and peppers are beginning to brown. Stir in the spice mixture and cook for 1 minute, stirring until the juices start to thicken.

5 Add the potatoes and nuts and heat very briefly to warm through. Transfer to serving plates and scatter with parsley to serve.

400 g (14 oz) new potatoes, scrubbed and cut into small chip-sized pieces
1 teaspoon cornflour
75 ml (3 fl oz) water
1 teaspoon ground coriander
1 teaspoon mixed dried herbs
½ teaspoon dried mint
4 teaspoons soy sauce
2 teaspoons vegan red or white wine vinegar
1 teaspoon vegan Dijon mustard
2 teaspoons light muscovado sugar
3 tablespoons vegetable oil or mild olive oil
25 g (1 oz) blanched almonds or cashew nuts, roughly chopped
1 green pepper, cored, deseeded and sliced
1 red pepper, cored, deseeded and sliced
1 yellow pepper, cored, deseeded and sliced
2 red onions, sliced
small handful of parsley, stalks removed and leaves finely chopped

Serves **2**
Prep time **20 minutes**
Cooking time **30 minutes**

AFFORDABILITY
2

# BEER-BATTERED ROOTS
## with Mushy Peas

**1** Cut the carrots and parsnips lengthways into thin wedges. Halve the onion and cut each half into 4 wedges so the root end keeps the wedges intact. Bring a saucepan of water to the boil and cook the vegetables for 2 minutes to soften slightly. Drain thoroughly.

**2** Cook the peas in boiling water for 3 minutes. Drain, return to the pan and mash well using a potato masher. Beat in the mint, dairy-free spread and 4 tablespoons of boiling water.

**3** For the batter, put the flour, baking powder and bouillon powder in a bowl. Make a well in the centre of the bowl and pour in half the beer. Beat with a whisk to make a smooth thick batter. Gradually whisk in the remaining beer.

**4** Sprinkle a little flour on to a large plate, add the carrots, parsnips and onions and turn in the flour to coat.

**5** Pour a 2.5 cm (1 inch) depth of oil into a large saucepan or frying pan and heat until a teaspoon of the batter sizzles on the surface. Add some of the vegetables to the batter, turning them until coated. Lift out and carefully lower into the oil with a slotted spoon. Fry for 3–4 minutes until the batter is crisp and turning pale golden. Lift out with the slotted spoon on to a plate lined with kitchen paper. Cook the remaining vegetables in the same way. Reheat the mushy peas and serve with the battered roots.

2 carrots, about 225 g (7½ oz)
2 small parsnips, about 225 g (7½ oz)
1 onion
200 g (7 oz) frozen peas
2 teaspoons finely chopped mint
1 tablespoon dairy-free spread
100 g (3½ oz) plain flour, plus extra for dusting
1 teaspoon baking powder
1 teaspoon vegan bouillon powder
200 ml (7 fl oz) vegan beer
vegetable oil, for frying
salt and pepper

Serves **2**
Prep time **25 minutes**
Cooking time **20 minutes**

# VEGAN DINNER PARTY

Whether your friends are vegan, or they love nothing more than tucking into a T-bone, there's no reason why you can't gather everyone around the dining table for a fabulous meat-free dinner. It's a good opportunity to showcase some interesting vegan recipes, and to introduce your mates to ingredients and creative combinations that they might not have encountered before.

Of course, a successful dinner party isn't all about the food – you need to invite friends who are all likely to get along. It's also important to check you've got enough chairs, crockery and cutlery for the number of people you're expecting: eating dinner with a dessert spoon, or sitting cross-legged on the living room floor with a plate of spaghetti, doesn't make for a relaxing evening.

## PLAN AHEAD

Once you've chosen your menu, check the cupboards and make a shopping list. It's worth checking with your mates to ensure that no one has any allergies or really doesn't like a particular ingredient. You should also double check that everyone knows it's a vegan meal – people often bring wine or chocolates as a thank you gift and your guests will be embarrassed if they turn up with non-vegan offerings.

On the day, get yourself prepared well ahead of your guests' arrival. Prepping and cooking food often takes longer than you estimate, especially if you're cooking something new. It's also good to get all the peeling, chopping and mixing out of the way so that you can relax and chat to your friends, rather than spending the entire evening in the kitchen. If you haven't hosted a dinner party before, the trick is to prepare a cold starter and cold dessert ahead of time, and keep them in the fridge. Alternatively, just serve plates of cold nibbles and dips as an appetiser, leaving you to concentrate on the main dish.

## LAID-BACK DINNER WITH FRIENDS

**Starter:** Tapenade Bruschetta (see page 42)

**Main:** Farro Burgers with Oven Chips (see page 163)

**Dessert:** Chocolate Mousse Cakes with Summer Berries (see page 206)

## ROMANTIC MEAL FOR TWO

**Starter:** Chilled Gazpacho (see page 35)

**Main:** Pea & Mint Pesto Fettuccine (see page 104)

**Dessert:** Ultra-rich Chocolate Stacks (see page 200)

## FILM OR SPORTS NIGHT SOFA SUPPER

**Starter:** Hot & Smoky Hummus (see page 88)

**Main:** Vegan Moussaka (see page 144)

**Dessert:** Raspberry, Pistachio & Rose Semifreddo (see page 211)

# THAI CHICKPEA BURGERS

1 Pulse together the spring onions, lemon grass, ginger, chilli, garlic and coriander in a food processor until finely chopped. Add the chickpeas and then pulse again until roughly blended.

2 Add the flour and season with salt and pepper, then process until the mixture forms a coarse thick paste. Shape the mixture into 4 burgers.

3 Heat the oil in a frying pan, add the burgers and fry for 2-3 minutes on each side until browned. Serve with a bean sprout and pepper salad if liked.

**VARIATION**
For Mexican bean burgers, pulse together 4 spring onions, 1 garlic clove, a handful of coriander leaves and 1 teaspoon each of chilli powder, ground cumin and ground coriander in a food processor. Add a drained 400 g (14 oz) can mixed beans and pulse again until roughly blended. Add 2 tablespoons of wholemeal plain flour and 3 tablespoons of natural soya yogurt and season with salt and pepper. Blend until the mixture forms a coarse thick paste. Shape into 4 burgers and fry as above. Serve in vegan buns with guacamole and tomato salsa.

4 spring onions
1 lemon grass stalk, outer leaves removed
1.5 cm (¾ inch) piece of fresh root ginger, peeled and chopped
1 red chilli, halved and deseeded
1 garlic clove, peeled
handful of coriander leaves
400 g (14 oz) can chickpeas, drained and rinsed
2 tablespoons wholemeal plain flour
3 tablespoons rapeseed oil
salt and pepper

Serves **4**
Prep time **20 minutes**
Cooking time **10 minutes**

AFFORDABILITY
1

# FARRO BURGERS
## *with oven chips*

AFFORDABILITY
2

**1** Put the farro and stock in a saucepan and bring to a simmer. Cook gently for about 15 minutes until the farro is very soft and most of the stock has been absorbed. Drain thoroughly through a sieve.

**2** Cut the potatoes into chunky chips, toss with 1 tablespoon of the oil and plenty of salt and pepper. Tip out on to a baking sheet and bake in a preheated oven, 220°C (425°F), Gas Mark 7 for 35–40 minutes until golden. Turn the potatoes once or twice with a fish slice during cooking.

**3** Heat another 1 tablespoon of the oil in a frying pan and fry the onion for 5 minutes. Add the carrots and fry for a further 5 minutes. Once cooled, tip into a food processor with the gherkins, herbs, almond butter, farro and plenty of black pepper and blend until the ingredients cling together but retain a little texture.

**4** Turn out on to the work surface and shape into a compact cake. Cut into 8 even-sized wedges. Shape each into a compact ball and flatten firmly into burger shapes.

**5** Heat the remaining oil in the frying pan and gently fry the cakes for about 3 minutes until golden on the underside. Carefully turn with a fish slice and cook for a further 2 minutes. Serve with the oven chips, vegan mayonnaise and tomato salad.

125 g (4 oz) quick-cook farro, rinsed
500 ml (18 fl oz) vegetable stock (see page 219)
1 kg (2 lb 4 oz) baking potatoes, scrubbed
4 tablespoons mild olive oil or vegetable oil
1 large onion, chopped
300 g (10 oz) carrots, coarsely grated
50 g (2 oz) gherkins, chopped
3 tablespoons chopped dill, tarragon or parsley
2 tablespoons almond butter
salt and pepper

**To serve**
vegan mayonnaise or Soyannaise (see page 218)
tomato salad

Serves **4**
Prep time **20 minutes**
Cooking time **1 hour 10 minutes**

# TOFU & CARAMELIZED ONION
# SAUSAGES
## with Cauliflower purée

4 tablespoons mild olive oil
3 red onions, chopped
1 teaspoon caster sugar
2 teaspoons chopped thyme
1 garlic clove, chopped
50 g (2 oz) vegan white or brown bread
200 g (7 oz) plain or olive-flavoured tofu
1 small cauliflower, cut into small florets
2 teaspoons cornflour
1½ teaspoons vegan bouillon powder
1 teaspoon balsamic vinegar
salt and pepper

Serves **2-3**
Prep time **30 minutes**
Cooking time **25 minutes**

AFFORDABILITY
**1**

1   Heat 2 tablespoons of the oil in a frying pan and add the onions and sugar. Fry gently, stirring frequently, until the onions are deep golden and tender, about 10 minutes. Transfer half to a plate and add the thyme and garlic to the pan. Fry for a further 1 minute.

2   Tear the bread into small pieces and put in a food processor or blender. Blend to make coarse breadcrumbs. Add the onion, thyme and garlic mixture and crumble in the tofu. Blend until the mixture is fine enough to hold together when a small amount is pressed into a ball.

3   Tip out on to the work surface and compact the mixture into a cake. Cut into 6 wedges and shape each into a sausage.

4   Cook the cauliflower in boiling water for 8 minutes, or until tender. Drain through a colander, reserving the liquid. Purée about two-thirds of the cauliflower and a dash of the cooking liquid in a food processor or high-speed blender until smooth. Season with salt and pepper and return the purée to the saucepan with the remaining cauliflower florets.

5   Heat the remaining oil in the frying pan and fry the sausages for 5 minutes, turning frequently until browned. Lift out and keep warm.

6   Blend the cornflour with a dash of water and make up to 300 ml (½ pint) with the cauliflower cooking liquid. Add to the pan with the reserved onions and the bouillon powder. Bring to the boil, stirring until thickened. Stir in the vinegar and season to taste. Gently reheat the cauliflower purée and serve with the tofu sausages and gravy.

# WALNUT & APPLE ROAST

1. Line a small loaf tin with a capacity of about 900 ml (1½ pints) with baking paper, pushing the paper into the corners.

2. Heat the oil in a frying pan and fry the fennel for 5 minutes. Add the walnuts and garlic and fry for a further 2 minutes.

3. Put the bread in a food processor and blend to make coarse crumbs. Tip in the walnut mixture and blend until the nuts are finely chopped. Peel, core and grate the apple into the mixture. Add the coriander, paprika, sugar and a little salt and blend very briefly to mix.

4. Pack firmly into the tin and level the surface. Bake in a preheated oven, 180°C (350°F), Gas Mark 4, for 30 minutes. Lift out of the tin, peel away the sides of the paper and return to the oven for a further 10 minutes. Leave to stand for 10 minutes.

5. In a small bowl combine the ketchup and balsamic vinegar. Thickly slice the nut roast and serve with the sauce.

3 tablespoons olive oil
1 large fennel bulb, chopped
200 g (7 oz) walnut pieces
3 garlic cloves, chopped
75 g (3 oz) vegan white or brown bread, torn into pieces
1 crisp dessert apple
15 g (½ oz) coriander, chopped
1 teaspoon ground paprika
2 teaspoons caster sugar
4 tablespoons tomato ketchup
2 tablespoons balsamic vinegar
salt and pepper

Serves **4**
Prep time **20 minutes**
Cooking time **50 minutes**

# LET'S BAKE

DATE & PRUNE BROWNIES

ALMOND, RASPBERRY & DATE BARS

PLUM, BANANA & APPLE CRUMBLES

HERB & WALNUT RYE SODA BREAD

# Chilli & Courgette FOCACCIA

1 Sift the flour into a bowl. Add the yeast to one side and the salt to the other side. Add 2 tablespoons of the oil and the measured water and mix to form a dough, adding a little more water if the dough seems dry.

2 Tip the dough on to a lightly floured surface and knead for 10 minutes until smooth and stretchy. Put the dough in a clean bowl, cover with clingfilm and leave to rise in a warm place for about 1 hour until doubled in size.

3 Turn the dough out on to a lightly floured surface and knead lightly for 1 minute. Press or roll the dough out to a rough rectangle about 1 cm (½ inch) thick and place on a lightly oiled baking sheet. Loosely cover and leave to prove for 20 minutes.

4 Meanwhile, heat 1 tablespoon of the remaining oil in a frying pan, add the onion and cook over a medium heat for about 3 minutes until just softened. Add the courgette and chilli and cook for a further 3 minutes. Set aside.

5 Use your fingertips to make indentations in the dough surface. Drizzle over the remaining oil and bake in a preheated oven, 200°C (400°F), Gas Mark 6, for 10 minutes. Scatter over the vegetable mixture with the salt flakes and rosemary sprigs and bake for a further 10-15 minutes until golden. Cool on a wire rack.

500 g (1 lb 2 oz) strong white bread flour, plus extra for dusting
7 g (¼ oz) sachet fast-action dried yeast
1 teaspoon salt
4 tablespoons olive oil, plus extra for oiling
275 ml (9 fl oz) warm water
½ small onion, thinly sliced
½ small courgette, trimmed and thinly sliced
1 red chilli, deseeded and thinly sliced
1 teaspoon sea salt flakes
few small rosemary sprigs

Serves **6**
Prep time **30 minutes, plus proving**
Cooking time **30-35 minutes**

AFFORDABILITY
1

# *Toasted* POTATO BREAD WITH TOMATOES

375 g (13 oz) potatoes, peeled and cut into chunks
1 teaspoon fast-action dried yeast
1 teaspoon caster sugar
1 tablespoon sunflower oil, plus extra for oiling
200 g (7 oz) strong white bread flour, plus extra for dusting
100 g (3½ oz) strong wholemeal bread flour
2 tablespoons chopped rosemary
1 tablespoon thyme leaves
salt and pepper

**Topping**
2 tablespoons olive oil
250 g (8 oz) cherry tomatoes (in a mix of colours), halved
½ teaspoon thyme leaves
½ teaspoon sea salt flakes

Serves **4**
Prep time **30 minutes**, plus proving and cooling
Cooking time **1 hour**

1 Cook the potato chunks in a large saucepan of lightly salted boiling water for 15-20 minutes until tender but not mushy. Drain really well, reserving the cooking liquid.

2 Put 6 tablespoons of the cooking liquid into a large bowl and leave to cool until lukewarm. Sprinkle over the yeast, then stir in the sugar and set aside for 10 minutes.

3 Mash the potatoes with the oil, then stir in the yeast mixture and mix well with a wooden spoon. Mix in the flours, herbs and salt and pepper, then turn out on to a lightly floured surface and knead well to incorporate the last of the flour. Knead the dough until soft and pliable, then put in a lightly oiled bowl, cover with clingfilm and leave to rise in a warm place for 1 hour until well risen.

4 Knead the dough on a lightly floured surface, then roughly shape it into a round, place on a baking sheet and lightly cover it with oiled clingfilm. Leave to prove in a warm place for 30 minutes. Score a cross into the dough with a sharp knife and bake in a preheated oven, 220°C (425°F), Gas Mark 7, for 35-40 minutes until well risen and crusty on top. Transfer to a wire rack to cool for 30 minutes.

5 Cut 4 slices of the bread and lightly toast. Meanwhile, heat the oil for the topping in a frying pan, add the tomatoes and cook over a high heat for 2-3 minutes until softened. Stir in the thyme and salt flakes. Serve with the toasted bread, seasoned with pepper.

AFFORDABILITY

# HERB & WALNUT RYE SODA BREAD

1 Mix together the flour, walnuts, mixed herbs, bicarbonate of soda, xanthan gum and salt in a large bowl, then make a well in the centre. Whisk together the rice milk and rapeseed oil in a jug, then pour into the well and stir in with a wooden spoon until a soft, slightly sticky dough is formed.

2 Turn the dough out on to a lightly floured surface and pat into an 18 cm (7 inch) round. Place on to a baking sheet. Scatter over the extra walnuts and gently press to adhere to the dough. Make a deep cross in the dough with a sharp knife, then leave to stand in a warm place for 30 minutes.

3 Bake in a preheated oven, 220°C (425°F), Gas Mark 7, for 40-45 minutes until the bread is crisp on the outside and cooked through - the base should sound hollow when tapped with the fingertips. Turn out on to a wire rack to cool before slicing thickly to serve.

## VARIATION

For pumpkin & sunflower seed wholemeal soda bread, mix together 250 g (8 oz) wholemeal plain flour, 1 teaspoon of bicarbonate of soda, 2 teaspoons of xanthan gum and 4 tablespoons each of sunflower seeds and pumpkin seeds in a large bowl. Make a well in the centre. Continue with the recipe as above, adding the rice milk and rapeseed oil to make a dough and preparing it on the baking sheet for baking. After cutting the cross in the dough, scatter with an extra tablespoon of pumpkin seeds and leave in a warm place for 30 minutes. Bake, cool and serve as above.

250 g (8 oz) rye flour
50 g (2 oz) walnuts, roughly chopped, plus 1 tablespoon roughly chopped for scattering
4 tablespoons chopped mixed herbs, such as rosemary, parsley or thyme
1 teaspoon bicarbonate of soda
2 teaspoons xanthan gum
¼ teaspoon salt
225 ml (8 fl oz) rice milk
25 ml (1 fl oz) rapeseed oil, plus extra for oiling

Serves **6**
Preparation time **15 minutes, plus standing**
Cooking time **40-45 minutes**

AFFORDABILITY

1

# *Vanilla & jam* SHORTBREAD

1. Beat the spread and caster sugar together in a bowl until pale and fluffy. Sift the flour and cornflour together into the mixture, add the vanilla and mix until combined. Roll the dough into a ball, wrap in clingfilm and chill for 30 minutes.

2. Roll the dough out on a lightly floured surface to about 5 mm (¼ inch) thick. Use a 5 cm (2 inch) square or round cutter to cut out 16 squares or rounds, rerolling the trimmings as necessary. Place on 2 baking sheets lined with baking paper and bake in a preheated oven, 160°C (325°F), Gas Mark 3, for 10-12 minutes until pale golden.

3. Leave the shortbreads to cool on the baking sheets for 10 minutes until firm, then transfer to a wire rack to cool completely.

4. Sandwich the biscuits together with the jam and dust with icing sugar.

**VARIATION**

For jam & coconut streusel tarts, make the shortbread dough and chill as above. Roll the dough out as above, then use a 7 cm (3 inch) round cutter to cut out 12 rounds, rerolling the trimmings as necessary. Use the rounds to line 12 holes of a bun tin. Add a teaspoonful of raspberry or strawberry jam to each lined hole. Put 25 g (1 oz) plain flour, 75 g (3 oz) caster sugar, 50 g (2 oz) dairy-free spread and 3 tablespoons of desiccated coconut in a bowl and rub together with your fingertips until crumbly. Sprinkle over the jam and bake in a preheated oven, 160°C (325°F), Gas Mark 3, for 15 minutes until golden.

125 g (4 oz) dairy-free spread
50 g (2 oz) caster sugar
150 g (5 oz) plain flour, plus extra
  for dusting
25 g (1 oz) cornflour
1 teaspoon vanilla extract
3 tablespoons raspberry or
  strawberry jam
icing sugar, for dusting

Makes **8**
Prep time **30 minutes,
  plus chilling**
Cooking time **10-12 minutes**

# ALMOND, RASPBERRY & DATE BARS

AFFORDABILITY 2

1 Heat the almond butter, agave syrup, margarine and demerara sugar in a saucepan over a very low heat, stirring constantly, until melted. Add the oats, flour, cinnamon and dates and mix well.

2 Transfer the mixture to a lightly oiled 18 × 28 cm (7 × 11 inch) shallow baking tin and level with the back of a metal spoon, slightly dampened to ease spreading.

3 With a teaspoon, make holes in the mixture and press in the raspberries, then scatter with the walnuts, sesame seeds and sunflower seeds. Bake in a preheated oven, 190°C (375°F), Gas Mark 5, for 15 minutes, or until the edges turn a pale golden brown.

4 Leave to cool in the tin for 10 minutes before scoring into 12 bars, then leave to cool completely before cutting the mixture into bars and carefully removing from the tin.

5 tablespoons crunchy almond butter
8 tablespoons agave syrup
50 g (2 oz) soya margarine
4 tablespoons demerara sugar
150 g (5 oz) rolled oats
2 tablespoons rice flour
½ teaspoon ground cinnamon
150 g (5 oz) fresh Medjool dates, pitted and chopped
110 g (4 oz) raspberries
25 g (1 oz) walnuts, roughly chopped
1 teaspoon sesame seeds
1 tablespoon sunflower seeds
sunflower oil, for oiling

Makes **12**
Prep time **10 minutes**
Cooking time **15 minutes**

# Sugar-free FRUIT GRANOLA BARS

1  Line a baking sheet with baking paper. Toss the apple with the lemon juice, agave syrup and cinnamon in a bowl, then spread out on the lined baking sheet and roast in a preheated oven, 160°C (325°F), Gas Mark 3, for 20 minutes. Remove from the oven and leave to cool.

2  Increase the oven temperature to 180°C (350°F), Gas Mark 4. Put all the ingredients for the granola in a food processor and pulse a few times until mixed. Fold in the cooled roasted apple. Lightly oil a 20 cm (8 inch) square shallow cake tin with the sunflower oil, spoon in the granola mixture and level with the back of a spoon. Bake in the oven for 20 minutes.

3  Leave to cool for 15 minutes before cutting into 9 squares to serve.

225 g (7½ oz) peeled, cored and roughly chopped dessert apples
1 tablespoon lemon juice
1 tablespoon agave syrup
½ teaspoon ground cinnamon
sunflower oil, for oiling

**Granola**
125 g (4 oz) rolled oats
125 g (4 oz) ready-to-eat dried apricots
125 g (4 oz) fresh Medjool dates, pitted and roughly chopped
2 tablespoons ground flaxseed (linseed)
2 tablespoons smooth peanut butter
55 ml (2 fl oz) agave syrup

Makes **9**
Prep time **20 minutes, plus cooling**
Cooking time **40 minutes**

AFFORDABILITY
2

# CRANBERRY SCONES
## & Compote

6 tablespoons soya milk
1 tablespoon cider vinegar
1 tablespoon ground golden
   flaxseed (linseed)
275 g (9 oz) plain flour, plus extra
   for dusting
50 g (2 oz) golden caster sugar
1 teaspoon baking powder
½ teaspoon bicarbonate of soda
1 teaspoon ground cinnamon
125 g (4 oz) dairy-free spread,
   cubed, plus extra for greasing
125 g (4 oz) dried cranberries
1 tablespoon demerara sugar

**Compote**

125 g (4 oz) strawberries, hulled
   and quartered
2 tablespoons caster sugar
125 g (4 oz) blackberries

Serves **6**
Prep time **20 minutes,**
   **plus standing and cooling**
Cooking time **25 minutes**

1 Mix 5 tablespoons of the soya milk, the vinegar and flaxseed together in a jug, then leave to stand for 10 minutes (the mixture will separate slightly and turn thick).

2 Meanwhile, heat the strawberries and sugar for the compote in a saucepan over a gentle heat for 2–3 minutes until the sugar has dissolved. Add the blackberries and cook for a further 2–3 minutes until the fruit has softened and a juice has formed. Remove from the heat and leave to cool.

3 Put the flour in a large bowl and stir in the caster sugar, baking powder, bicarbonate of soda and cinnamon. Add the dairy-free spread and rub in with your fingertips until the mixture resembles fine breadcrumbs. Stir in the cranberries, then add the soya milk mixture and mix to form a soft dough.

4 Roll the dough out on a lightly floured work surface to an 18 cm (7 inch) round and score into 6 wedges with a knife. Place on a lightly greased baking sheet, brush with the remaining soya milk and sprinkle with the demerara sugar.

5 Bake in a preheated oven, 200°C (400°F), Gas Mark 6, for 15–18 minutes until golden and cooked through. Leave to cool slightly, then serve warm with the cooled compote.

**VARIATION**

For lemon & blueberry scones, finely grate the zest of 1 lemon, then squeeze the juice. Mix 5 tablespoons of soya milk, 1 tablespoon of ground golden flaxseed and the lemon juice together in a jug, then leave to stand for 10 minutes. Make the dough as above, stirring in the lemon zest and 125 g (4 oz) blueberries in place of the cranberries. Roll out on a lightly floured surface to a 20 cm (8 inch) round and score into 6 wedges. Place on a lightly greased baking sheet and bake as above. Serve warm.

# Peach, Apricot & Fig
# CRUMBLE

**Crumble**

125 g (4 oz) plain wholemeal flour
2 tablespoons rapeseed oil
2 tablespoons sweetened soya
  milk
25 g (1 oz) porridge oats
50 g (2 oz) dark brown sugar
25 g (1 oz) flaked almonds
250 g (8 oz) peaches, pitted and
  sliced
250 g (8 oz) ready-to-eat dried
  apricots, chopped
6 fresh or dried figs, diced
juice of 1 lime
¼ teaspoon ground nutmeg
1 teaspoon ground cinnamon

**Custard**

2 tablespoons vegan custard
  powder or cornflour
3 tablespoons maple syrup
600 ml (1 pint) oat milk or soya
  milk

Serves **6**
Prep time **15 minutes**
Cooking time **30 minutes**

1 Pour the flour into a large bowl and lightly mix in the oil
and the soya milk with a fork until the mixture forms coarse
crumbs. Stir the oats, sugar and almonds into the mixture.

2 Place the fruit in a 1.2 litre (2 pint) ovenproof dish and
sprinkle it with about 4 tablespoons of water, the lime juice,
nutmeg and cinnamon.

3 Spoon the crumble mixture over the fruit and bake in a
preheated oven, 180°C (350°F), Gas Mark 4, for 25-30
minutes until golden brown.

4 Put the custard powder in a jug, add the maple syrup and
4 tablespoons of the oat milk and stir together well.

5 Heat the remaining milk in a small saucepan until hot but not
boiling, then remove from the heat and gradually stir in the
custard powder mixture to thicken. Return the pan to a
medium heat and cook for a few minutes, stirring constantly.

6 Serve the crumble with the hot custard.

# PLUM, BANANA & APPLE
# CRUMBLES
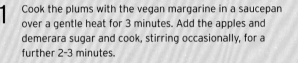

6 plums, halved and pitted
50 g (2 oz) vegan margarine
2 dessert apples, peeled, cored
  and cut into chunks
2 tablespoons demerara sugar
2 bananas, cut into chunks
½ teaspoon ground cinnamon
pinch of ground allspice (optional)

## Crumble
100 g (3½ oz) plain flour
50 g (2 oz) vegan margarine,
  cubed
4 tablespoons demerara sugar
4 tablespoons rolled oats

Serves **4**
Prep time **15 minutes**
Cooking time **30 minutes**

**1** Cook the plums with the vegan margarine in a saucepan over a gentle heat for 3 minutes. Add the apples and demerara sugar and cook, stirring occasionally, for a further 2–3 minutes.

**2** Remove the pan from the heat, add the bananas and spices and toss gently to lightly coat all the fruit in the sugar and spices. Divide the mixture between 4 × 250 ml (8 fl oz) gratin dishes.

**3** Put the flour for the crumble in a bowl, add the margarine and rub in with your fingertips until the mixture resembles fine breadcrumbs. Stir in the sugar and oats.

**4** Spoon evenly over the top of the fruit in each dish, place the dishes on a baking sheet and then bake in a preheated oven, 200°C (400°F), Gas Mark 6, for 20 minutes until the crumble is golden and the fruit is bubbling. Serve with natural soya yogurt if liked.

AFFORDABILITY 1

# Date & Prune BROWNIES

250 g (8 oz) wholemeal flour
250 ml (8 fl oz) rice milk or water
50 ml (2 fl oz) soya milk
50 ml (2 fl oz) rapeseed oil
3 tablespoons cocoa powder
1 tablespoon carob powder
250 g (8 oz) dark brown sugar
1 teaspoon salt
1 teaspoon vanilla extract
125 g (4 oz) ready-to-eat dried
 prunes, pitted
50 g (2 oz) medjool dates, pitted
1½ teaspoons baking powder
1 tablespoon ground almonds

Makes **8-10**
Prep time **15 minutes**
Cooking time **25-35 minutes**

AFFORDABILITY
1

**1** Line a 27 × 17 × 3.5 cm (10½ × 6½ × 1½ inch) baking tin with baking paper and oil lightly.

**2** Place 2 heaped tablespoons of the flour in a saucepan and mix in the rice milk. Cook, stirring constantly, over a medium heat until thick. Set aside to cool completely.

**3** Combine the soya milk, oil, cocoa and carob in a bowl and stir until smooth.

**4** Transfer the cooled flour mixture to a food processer or liquidizer, add the sugar, salt, vanilla, prunes and dates and blend until smooth. Add the cocoa mixture and blend again.

**5** In a bowl mix the remaining flour with the baking powder and the ground almonds, then add to the prune mixture and blend again.

**6** Pour the mixture into the prepared tin and bake for 25-35 minutes in an oven preheated to 180°C (350°F), Gas Mark 4, until firm to the touch.

**7** Cut into slices and serve hot with a scoop of vegan ice cream and some grated dairy-free chocolate.

# CHOCOLATE CHIP
# BISCUITS

1 Line a baking sheet with baking paper and grease with coconut oil.

2 Put the flour, sugar, cinnamon, carob powder, salt and dates into a bowl and mix well. Add the milk, oil and vanilla extract and beat with an electric mixer or fork. Stir in the orange zest and chocolate.

3 Place 12 spoonfuls of the mixture on the prepared baking sheet and smooth the tops with a wet knife.

4 Bake the biscuits for 10 minutes in a preheated oven, 180°C (350°F), Gas Mark 4, then cool on a wire rack. Store in an airtight container until needed.

coconut oil, for greasing
125 g (4 oz) self-raising wholemeal flour or 125 g (4 oz) plain flour plus 1 teaspoon baking powder
50 g (2 oz) soft brown sugar
1 teaspoon ground cinnamon
4 teaspoons carob powder
pinch of salt
50 g (2 oz) finely chopped dates
100 ml (3½ fl oz) sweetened soya milk
75 ml (3 fl oz) rapeseed oil
1 teaspoon vanilla extract
1 teaspoon finely grated orange zest
25 g (1 oz) dairy-free chocolate or carob, coarsely grated or chopped

Makes **12**
Prep time **10 minutes**
Cooking time **10 minutes**

## STUDENT TIP

**COMPARE PRICES** Thanks to the internet, you can now compare the price of your grocery shop down to the last peanut. Shop with your head, not your heart, and take your custom to the supermarket with the best prices.

AFFORDABILITY

# STEM GINGER & DARK CHOCOLATE BISCUITS

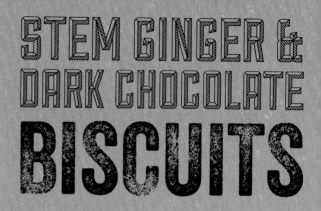

6 tablespoons golden syrup
50 g (2 oz) dairy-free spread
115 g (4 oz) rolled oats
75 g (3 oz) wholemeal plain flour
1 teaspoon baking powder
50 g (2 oz) well-drained stem ginger in syrup, finely chopped
50 g (2 oz) plain dark dairy-free chocolate (70% cocoa solids), roughly chopped

Makes **14**
Prep time **20 minutes**
Cooking time **15 minutes**

**1** Heat the golden syrup and dairy-free spread in a small saucepan over a gentle heat until melted, stirring. Allow to cool slightly.

**2** Mix all the remaining ingredients together in a large bowl. Pour in the syrup mixture and mix to form a soft dough. Place 14 spoonfuls of the mixture well spaced apart on a large baking sheet lined with baking paper and gently press with the back of a spoon to flatten slightly.

**3** Bake in a preheated oven, 180°C (350°F), Gas Mark 4, for 8–10 minutes until pale golden.

**4** Leave the biscuits to cool on the baking sheet for 5 minutes until firm, then transfer to a wire rack to cool completely.

## STUDENT TIP

**CUT YOUR COFFEE COSTS** Buy a reusable coffee cup and make your own hot drink before leaving the house. This could save you a small fortune over the year on pricey cafeteria cappuccinos, and shrink your carbon footprint.

# ALL THINGS SWEET

RAW CHOCOLATE MUD PIE

CHEWY CHERRY BITES

RASPBERRY, PISTACHIO
& ROSE SEMIFREDDO

WATERMELON & LIME
GRENADINE SQUARES

# CHARGRILLED FRUIT
## with chilli salt

1    Cut the mango into 2 cm (¾ inch) pieces and cut the pineapple into small wedges. Skewer the fruit on to metal or wooden skewers (if using wooden skewers, pre-soak them for 30 minutes), alternating the fruits.

2    Mix together the chilli and salt and set aside.

3    Preheat a griddle pan to medium heat and grill the skewers on each side for 3 minutes until golden and caramelized. Remove the skewers from the heat, sprinkle with the salt chilli mix and serve.

1 large mango, peeled and stoned
½ pineapple, peeled
2 bananas
½ teaspoon crushed dried chilli
1 tablespoon sea salt

Serves **6-8**
Prep time **15 minutes**
Cooking time **10 minutes**

## STUDENT TIP

**SHOP LATE** Many supermarkets seriously knock down their prices just before closing time. And although 24-hour trading has cut down on this to a certain extent, you can still grab a bargain if you head to the shops after hours.

AFFORDABILITY
1

# STUFFED
## SPICE-ROASTED
# PEARS

1 Halve the pears and then remove a small slice from the back of each so that they sit level in a roasting tin. Scoop out the core and seeds, leaving the stalk intact.

2 Mix the prunes and hazelnuts with the cinnamon and maple syrup in a bowl, then fold in the blackberries.

3 Pile the mixture into the pear cavities and top each with a small knob of the dairy-free spread. Cover the roasting tin with foil and bake in a preheated oven, 200°C (400°F), Gas Mark 6, for 25 minutes.

4 Remove the foil and roast for a further 10 minutes. Serve with the juices spooned over the pears along with a scoop of soya ice cream or soya yogurt, if liked.

**VARIATION**
For stuffed roasted apples with agave syrup, cut 4 apples in half and scoop out the core, leaving the stalk intact. Remove a small slice from the back of each apple half so that it sits level in a roasting tin. Mix 2 roughly chopped dried figs and 25 g (1 oz) lightly roasted Marcona almonds with 4 tablespoons of agave syrup in a bowl, then fold in 50 g (2 oz) raspberries. Spoon into the apple cavities and cover the tin with foil. Bake and then serve as above.

4 ripe pears
3 ready-to-eat pitted prunes, roughly chopped
25 g (1 oz) roasted hazelnuts, roughly chopped
½ teaspoon ground cinnamon
4 tablespoons maple syrup
75 g (3 oz) blackberries, halved
25 g (1 oz) dairy-free spread

Serves **4**
Prep time **20 minutes**
Cooking time **35 minutes**

AFFORDABILITY
1

# POACHED PEACHES
## & RASPBERRIES

1 Pour the measured water and marsala or sherry into a saucepan, then add the sugar. Slit the vanilla pod lengthways and scrape out the black seeds from inside the pod. Add these to the water with the pod, then gently heat the mixture until the sugar has dissolved.

2 Place the peach halves in an ovenproof dish so that they sit together snugly. Pour over the hot syrup, then cover and cook in a preheated oven, 180°C (350°F), Gas Mark 4, for 20 minutes.

3 Scatter over the raspberries. Serve the fruit either warm or cold. Spoon into serving bowls and decorate with the vanilla pod cut into thin strips.

250 ml (8 fl oz) water
150 ml (¼ pint) marsala or sweet sherry
75 g (3 oz) caster sugar
1 vanilla pod
6 peaches, halved and pitted
150 g (5 oz) fresh raspberries

Serves **6**
Preparation time **15 minutes**
Cooking time **25 minutes**

AFFORDABILITY
3

# MULLED WINE
## Pears

300 ml (½ pint) cheap vegan
   red wine
200 ml (7 fl oz) water
rind and juice of 1 orange
1 cinnamon stick, broken into large
   pieces
6 cloves
2 small fresh bay leaves
75 g (3 oz) caster sugar
6 pears
3 teaspoons cornflour

Serves **6**
Prep time **10 minutes**
Cooking time **12 minutes**

1 Pour the wine and measured water into a saucepan that will
hold the pears snugly. Cut the orange rind into thin strips,
then add to the pan with the orange juice, spices, bay
leaves and sugar. Heat gently until the sugar has dissolved.

2 Peel the pears, leaving the stalks on, then add them to the
red wine syrup. Simmer gently for 10 minutes, turning the
pears several times so that they cook and colour evenly.

3 Lift the pears out of the pan and put on a plate. Mix the
cornflour with a little water in a cup, then stir into the wine
syrup and bring to the boil, stirring until thickened and
smooth. Add the pears and leave to cool.

4 Transfer to shallow dishes with a rim and serve.

# APRICOT & PAPAYA FOOL

150 g (5 oz) ready-to-eat dried
  apricots, chopped
25 g (1 oz) dried papaya, chopped
450 ml (¾ pint) sweetened soya
  milk
2 tablespoons flax oil
6 strawberries or 1 kiwi fruit, to
  decorate

Serves **6**
Prep time **5 minutes, plus
  soaking and chilling**

1 Soak the dried apricots and papaya in the soya milk
overnight.

2 Transfer the dried fruit and soya milk to a food processor
or liquidizer and blend to a smooth consistency. Add the oil
and blend again.

3 Divide the mixture between 6 small glass dishes, then
refrigerate until set.

4 Decorate each serving with a sliced strawberry or some
slivers of kiwi fruit. Serve with coconut cream, if liked.

AFFORDABILITY
2

# Chewy Cherry BITES

1 Line a 12 cm (4½ inch) square container with clingfilm.

2 Put the dates and oats in a food processor and process to fine crumbs. Add the blueberries, cranberries, goji berries, chia seeds and vinegar and process again until the mixture starts to clump together.

3 Turn the mixture into the prepared container and press down firmly in an even layer using your hands. Let stand for 2-3 hours to firm up slightly. Serve cut into 9 small squares.

100 g (3½ oz) pitted dates
50 g (2 oz) jumbo rolled oats
75 g (3 oz) dried blueberries
75 g (3 oz) dried cranberries
25 g (1 oz) goji berries
4 tablespoons chia seeds
1 teaspoon apple cider vinegar

Makes **9**
Prep time **10 minutes, plus standing**

# COCONUT BALLS

250 g (8 oz) grated fresh
coconut, or desiccated coconut
softened with a little cold water
300 g (10 oz) sugar
300 ml (½ pint) water
a few drops of food colouring of
your choice (optional)

Makes **12**
Preparation time **15 minutes,
plus cooling and setting**
Cooking time **20 minutes**

1 Mix the coconut, sugar and measured water together. For coloured balls, divide the mixture between 2, 3 or more dishes (one for each colour) and add a drop or two of food colouring to each. If you want white coconut balls, do not add any food colouring.

2 One at a time, stir each mixture in a clean saucepan over a low heat until the syrup has almost all evaporated.

3 Put tablespoonfuls of the mixtures on a baking sheet lined with greaseproof paper, shaping each spoonful into a ball as you go. Once all the mixture has been used, you should have 12 coconut balls.

4 Allow to cool for about 1 hour to harden the outside a little, leaving the insides soft.

### VARIATION

For sticky coconut sauce, follow the method as above, adding an extra ⅛ teaspoon of salt and cooking over a low heat until a sticky caramel sauce has formed. Do not let it thicken to a point where it will harden. Use this sauce over black sticky rice or steamed sticky rice with coconut milk.

AFFORDABILITY
1

# ALMOND & WALNUT

125 g (4 oz) almonds
75 g (3 oz) walnuts
50 g (2 oz) coconut oil
1 banana
1 teaspoon vanilla extract
2 tablespoons almond butter
3 tablespoons coconut blossom
  nectar
2 large pitted dates
good pinch of sea salt

Makes **15**
Prep time **10 minutes, plus
  soaking and freezing**

1 Put the almonds and walnuts in separate bowls, cover with cold water and let them soak for several hours or overnight.

2 Put the coconut oil in a small heatproof bowl and stand it in a larger heatproof bowl of boiling water. Let melt.

3 Line a small container, about 15 cm (6 inches) square, with clingfilm.

4 Thoroughly drain the nuts, keeping them separate. Chop the walnuts and set aside.

5 Transfer the almonds to a food processor and process until finely ground. Chop the banana into the processor and add the melted coconut oil, vanilla extract, almond butter, coconut blossom nectar, dates and salt. Process again to a thick paste. Remove the blade and stir in the walnuts by hand.

6 Turn the mixture into the prepared container, level the surface and press down firmly. Freeze for about 1 hour until firm. Serve cut into small squares.

# Watermelon & Lime GRENADINE SQUARES

1 Place the grenadine, sugar and lime zest and juice with the measured water in a small saucepan and bring to the boil. Reduce the heat and cook gently for 6-8 minutes until thick and syrupy. Remove from the heat and allow to cool.

2 Meanwhile halve the watermelon and, using a sharp knife, slice the rind from the bottom of each half.

3 Lay the halves on a cutting board and, working from top to bottom, trim the rind from the watermelon flesh in 4 cuts, creating 2 large squares.

4 Cut each square of watermelon into equal bite-sized squares and place on a serving platter to form a neat large square (made up of the bite-sized squares).

5 Drizzle over the cooled grenadine syrup, scatter over the lime zest and serve immediately.

4 tablespoons grenadine
50 g (2 oz) caster sugar
finely grated zest and juice of
  1 lime, plus extra lime zest to
  decorate
100 ml (3½ fl oz) water
1 small-medium watermelon

Serves **4**
Prep time **20 minutes**

AFFORDABILITY 1

# Blueberry & Pear SLUMP

2 large ripe pears, peeled, cored
  and chopped
200 g (7 oz) blueberries
5 tablespoons caster sugar
175 g (6 oz) plain flour
1 teaspoon baking powder
50 g (2 oz) ground almonds
25 g (1 oz) dairy-free spread, diced
150 ml (5 fl oz) almond milk
25 g (1 oz) flaked almonds

Serves **4**
Prep time **20 minutes**
Cooking time **25-30 minutes**

1 Divide the pears and blueberries between 4 large ramekins and sprinkle with 2 tablespoons of the sugar.

2 Sift the flour and baking powder together into a bowl and stir in the ground almonds and 2 tablespoons of the remaining sugar. Add the spread and rub in with your fingertips. Stir in the almond milk to make a sticky dough.

3 Dot small spoonfuls of the dough over the fruit and sprinkle over the remaining tablespoon of sugar and the flaked almonds. Bake in a preheated oven, 190°C (375°F), Gas Mark 5, for 25-30 minutes until the fruit is soft and the topping is golden.

AFFORDABILITY
**1**

## STUDENT TIP

**SEPARATE SHELF** Chances are you'll need to buy a lot of separate food items (non-dairy spreads, cheese and yogurts, for example), so keep a shelf in the fridge and storecupboard that's dedicated to vegan food. That way, there won't be any foodie mix ups.

# COCONUT
## RICE PUDDING

1 Put the rice in a saucepan with the sugar and coconut milk. Refill the coconut milk can with water and add to the pan.

2 Bring the mixture to the boil, stirring, then pour into a shallow 1.5 litre (2½ pint) ovenproof dish. Bake in a preheated oven, 150°C (300°F), Gas Mark 2, for 1 hour 25 minutes, stirring occasionally, until the rice is tender and the liquid is absorbed.

3 Mix the mango and lime zest and juice together in a bowl and serve with the warm or cold rice pudding.

**VARIATION**

For coconut rice pudding brûlée, bring the rice, sugar, coconut milk and water to the boil, stirring, as above, then leave to simmer on the hob, stirring occasionally, for 20 minutes until the rice is tender and the liquid is absorbed. Spoon the mixture into individual heatproof ramekins, level the surface and leave to cool. Chill for 2-3 hours or overnight. Just before serving, sprinkle 1 tablespoon of demerara sugar evenly over the surface of each dish. Place under a hot grill or use a cook's blowtorch to melt and caramelize the sugar. Leave to cool for 10 minutes to harden the caramel before serving with chopped mango or rhubarb compote.

75 g (3 oz) Thai fragrant or pudding rice
50 g (2 oz) caster sugar
400 ml (14 fl oz) can coconut milk
1 ripe mango, peeled, stoned and chopped
finely grated zest and juice of 1 lime

Serves **4**
Prep time **15 minutes**
Cooking time **1½ hours**

# RAW GINGERBREAD BISCUITS

100 g (3½ oz) pecans, plus 15
   pecan halves to decorate
100 g (3½ oz) raisins
125 g (4 oz) rolled oats
4 tablespoons coconut palm sugar
1 teaspoon ground ginger
1 teaspoon mixed spice
¼ teaspoon ground cloves
good pinch of hot chilli powder

Makes **15**
Prep time **15 minutes, plus
   soaking and standing**

**1** Put the pecans in a bowl, cover with cold water and let soak for several hours or overnight. Drain and pat dry with kitchen paper.

**2** Transfer the nuts to a food processor, add the raisins and 100 g (3½ oz) of the oats, and process until the mixture forms fine crumbs. Add the coconut palm sugar and spices, then process again until the dough starts to clump together. Add the remaining oats and pulse briefly to combine.

**3** Divide the dough into 15 pieces, then shape into balls. Using a 5 cm (2 inch) biscuit cutter, cut biscuits out of the dough, and press a pecan half into the centre of each one. Repeat with the remaining balls. Serve immediately or store in an airtight container for several days.

AFFORDABILITY
2

# RAW SALTED PECAN BROWNIES

1 Put the pecans in a bowl, cover with cold water and let soak for several hours or overnight.

2 Line a 6 inch (15 cm) square shallow baking tin or similar-sized container with clingfilm or baking paper.

3 Drain the nuts and pat dry with kitchen paper, then transfer to a food processor and process briefly until chopped. Remove half the nuts and set aside.

4 Continue to process the remaining nuts until finely ground. Add the dates, maple syrup, cacao powder and salt and process thoroughly, scraping down the mixture from the sides of the bowl, until it forms a thick paste. Add the reserved chopped nuts and pulse briefly until combined. Turn the mixture into the prepared tin and press down firmly.

5 To make the topping, wipe out the processor, add the dates and salt and process to a paste. Add the maple syrup and enough of the measured water to form a spreadable paste.

6 Lift the brownie slab out of the tin and peel away the clingfilm or paper. Spread over the topping, cut into 16 small squares and serve.

150 g (5 oz) pecans
400 g (14 oz) pitted dates, coarsely chopped
50 ml (2 fl oz) maple syrup
65 g (2½ oz) cacao powder
good pinch of salt

**Topping**
100 g (3½ oz) pitted dates, coarsely chopped
½ teaspoon sea salt
1 tablespoon maple syrup
3-4 tablespoons water

Makes **16**
Prep time **10 minutes, plus soaking**

AFFORDABILITY
2

# ULTRA-RICH CHOCOLATE STACKS

150 g (5 oz) plain dark, dairy-free
  chocolate (90% cocoa solids),
  broken into pieces
125 ml (4 fl oz) coconut cream
1 tablespoon mint leaves
125 g (4 oz) raspberries
½ teaspoon cocoa powder
½ teaspoon icing sugar

Serves **4**
Prep time **20 minutes,
  plus chilling**

**1** Put the chocolate into a heatproof bowl and set over
a saucepan of hot water. Make sure the base of the bowl
does not touch the water, or the chocolate will burn. Stir
until melted.

**2** Line a baking sheet with baking paper and spoon
12 spoonfuls of the melted chocolate onto the sheet. Allow
the chocolate to spread into about 7 cm (3 inch) discs, then
refrigerate for 30 minutes until set.

**3** Whip the coconut cream in a bowl until thick. Place a
chocolate disc on to a serving plate and spoon some
coconut cream, mint leaves and raspberries on top. Place
another chocolate disc on top and spoon some more
coconut cream, mint leaves and raspberries on top. Finish
with a third chocolate disc. Repeat with the remaining
chocolate discs.

**4** Mix the cocoa and icing sugar together, then sift over the
chocolate stacks to serve.

**VARIATION**
For chocolate & orange stacks, melt the chocolate as above,
then stir in the finely grated zest of 1 orange. Spoon on to a lined
baking sheet and refrigerate until set as above. Whip the coconut
cream as above, then use to layer the discs in stacks of 3 along
with a well-drained 300 g (10 oz) can mandarin segments in juice.
Dust with cocoa powder to serve.

# BANANA FRITTERS
## & cinnamon sugar

AFFORDABILITY
1

1 Mix the flour, nutmeg and 1 teaspoon of the cinnamon together in a bowl, then make a well in the centre. Gradually add and whisk in enough of the sparkling water to make a smooth batter thick enough to coat the back of a spoon. Leave to stand for 20 minutes.

2 Fill a deep-sided saucepan one-third full with oil and heat to 180-190°C (350-375°F), or until a cube of bread browns in 30 seconds.

3 Using a pair of tongs, dip the banana pieces, in batches, into the batter, gently lower into the hot oil and cook for between 30 seconds and 1 minute until golden and crisp. Take care not to overcrowd the pan with too many at a time, as they will stick together and the oil temperature will drop.

4 Remove from the pan with a slotted spoon and drain on kitchen paper.

5 Mix the sugars with the remaining cinnamon, then scatter over the hot fritters to serve.

225 g (7½ oz) plain flour
½ teaspoon ground nutmeg
2 teaspoons ground cinnamon
375 ml (13 fl oz) sparkling water
sunflower oil, for deep-frying
4 bananas, halved both
   lengthways and widthways
3 tablespoons demerara sugar
1 tablespoon caster sugar

Serves **4**
Prep time **20 minutes,**
   **plus standing**
Cooking time **5 minutes**

# *Raw* BANOFFEE PIE

1 Put all the nuts in a bowl, cover with cold water and let soak for several hours or overnight.

2 Thoroughly drain the nuts, then transfer to a food processor. Add the hemp seeds and process until finely ground. Add 100 g (3½ oz) of the dates and a pinch of salt and process again until the mixture starts to cling together.

3 Tip into a 21–22 cm (8¼–8½ inch) loose-bottom flan tin. Using the back of a spoon, press the mixture firmly up the sides and into the bottom of the tin. Chill.

4 Meanwhile, put the remaining dates in a blender with the coconut water, vanilla extract and a pinch of salt and blend to a thick, smooth paste. Press 2 tablespoons of the paste through a sieve to extract as much pulp as possible, scraping the mixture from the bottom of the sieve, then mix with the maple syrup to make a purée. Set aside the paste and the purée.

5 Toss the bananas with the lemon juice. Arrange two-thirds over the base and spread with the date paste.

6 Scrape off the top thick layer of coconut cream into a bowl. Discard 1 tablespoon of the water left in each tin, then add the remaining water to the bowl. Beat until thickened and softly peaking. Beat in the agave syrup, then spread over the filling.

7 Scatter with the remaining bananas and drizzle with the reserved date purée. Chill until ready to serve.

75 g (3 oz) Brazil nuts
75 g (3 oz) almonds
4 tablespoons hemp seeds
300 g (10 oz) pitted dates
125 ml (4 fl oz) coconut water
2 teaspoons vanilla extract
1 tablespoon maple syrup
3 large or 4 medium bananas, sliced
1 tablespoon lemon juice
320 g (11½ oz) coconut cream, chilled overnight
2 tablespoons agave syrup
sea salt

Serves **8**
Prep time **25 minutes, plus overnight chilling and soaking**

# RAW STRAWBERRY & VANILLA
# CHEESECAKE

AFFORDABILITY
2

1. Put the almonds and cashew nuts in separate bowls, cover with cold water and let soak for several hours or overnight.

2. Thoroughly drain the almonds, then transfer to a food processor and process until finely chopped. Add the dates and coconut flour and process again until it is the consistency of finely ground biscuits and starts to cling together.

3. Using the back of a spoon, press the mixture firmly into the bottom and slightly up the sides of a 20 cm (8 inch) loose-bottomed cake tin. Chill.

4. Meanwhile, put the coconut oil in a small heatproof bowl and stand it in a larger heatproof bowl of boiling water. Let it melt.

5. Thoroughly drain the cashew nuts. Split the vanilla pod open and scrape out the seeds with the tip of a knife. Put the vanilla seeds in a food processor with the cashew nuts and coconut water and process until smooth, scraping down the mixture from the sides of the bowl.

6. Add the melted coconut oil, agave syrup and lemon juice and process again until pale and smooth.

7. Arrange half the strawberries over the almond base. Spoon half the cashew filling on top and spread level. Scatter over the remaining strawberries, then top with the remaining filling and spread level.

8. Freeze for 3-4 hours to firm up. Loosen the edges of the cheesecake and remove from the tin. Transfer to a serving plate while still semi-frozen and let soften in the refrigerator for a couple of hours, or until ready to serve. Serve decorated with extra strawberries.

125 g (4 oz) almonds
300 g (10 oz) cashew nuts
150 g (5 oz) pitted dates
3 tablespoons coconut flour
75 g (2¾ oz) coconut oil
1 vanilla pod
300 ml (½ pint) coconut water
75 ml (3 fl oz) agave syrup
1 tablespoon lemon juice
300 g (10 oz) strawberries, hulled
   and thinly sliced, plus extra to
   serve

Serves **8-10**
Prep time **25 minutes,**
   **plus soaking and chilling**

# RAW
## CHOCOLATE
## MUD PIE

1  Put the cashew nuts and hazelnuts in separate bowls, cover with cold water and let soak for several hours or overnight. Thoroughly drain the nuts, keeping them separate.

2  Transfer 125 g (4 oz) of the hazelnuts to a food processor and process until chopped. Add 150 g (5 oz) of the apricots and the cinnamon and process again until the mixture starts to stick together.

3  Tip into a 20 cm (8 inch) loose-bottomed flan tin. Using the back of a spoon, press the mixture firmly up the sides and into the bottom of the tin. Chill.

4  Meanwhile, put the cacao butter in a small heatproof bowl and stand it in a larger heatproof bowl of boiling water. Let melt.

5  Put the cashew nuts, almond milk, vanilla, cacao powder and agave syrup in a food processor and process until completely smooth, scraping down the mixture from the sides of the bowl. Add the melted cacao butter and process to combine. Turn on to the base and spread level. Freeze for 30 minutes or chill for 2-3 hours until firm.

6  Chop the remaining hazelnuts and apricots and scatter over the pie. Blend together the remaining cacao powder and agave syrup in a bowl to make a smooth syrup.

7  Transfer the pie to a plate and drizzle with the syrup to serve.

200 g (7 oz) cashew nuts
150 g (5 oz) hazelnuts
225 g (7½ oz) plump dried apricots
1 teaspoon ground cinnamon
50 g (2 oz) cacao butter
200 ml (7 fl oz) almond milk
1 vanilla pod, chopped into small pieces
50 g (2 oz) cacao powder, plus 1 tablespoon
100 ml (3½ fl oz) agave syrup, plus 3 tablespoons

Serves **8-10**
Prep time **20 minutes, plus chilling and soaking**

AFFORDABILITY 2

# CHOCOLATE MOUSSE CAKES
## WITH SUMMER BERRIES

1  Cut 6 squares of baking paper, each one 15 cm (6 inch). Press a square over an upturned dariole mold, creasing it down the sides to fit. Lift away and push the paper into the mould to form a lining. (Creasing it over the outside of the mould first makes it easier to fit neatly inside.) Repeat to line 5 more moulds. Alternatively, line 6 sections of a cupcake tin with paper cupcake cups.

2  Put the coconut oil in a small heatproof bowl and stand it in a larger heatproof bowl of boiling water. Let melt.

3  Put the avocados, cacao powder, agave syrup, vanilla extract and lemon juice in a food processor and process until smooth, scraping down the mixture from the sides of the bowl. Add the melted coconut oil and process again. Spoon the mixture into the prepared moulds or cups and chill for several hours or overnight. Top the cakes with the raspberries and blueberries or blackberries and serve.

75 g (3 oz) coconut oil
2 ripe avocados
50 g (2 oz) cacao powder
100 ml (3½ fl oz) agave syrup
2 teaspoons vanilla extract
squeeze of lemon juice
50 g (2 oz) raspberries
50 g (2 oz) blueberries or halved blackberries

Makes **6**
Prep time **25 minutes, plus chilling**

# RAW CARROT CAKE
## *with lime cashew frosting*

1   Put the cashew nuts in a bowl, cover with cold water and let soak for several hours or overnight.

2   Line 2 × 15 cm (6 inch) round cake tins with clingfilm.

3   Finely grate the carrots and pat dry between several thicknesses of kitchen paper.

4   Put the pineapple and spices into a food processor and process until chopped. Add the figs and process again until the mixture starts to cling together. Tip in the carrots, raisins and oatmeal and process until evenly combined.

5   Divide between the prepared tins and press down firmly. Chill for several hours or freeze for 30 minutes to firm up.

6   To make the frosting, thoroughly drain the nuts, then transfer to a food processor, add the almond milk and process until smooth. Add the maple syrup, lime zest and juice and thoroughly process until very thick, spreadable, and smooth, frequently scraping down the mixture from the sides of the bowl.

7   Carefully turn one of the carrot cakes out on to a flat serving plate and peel away the clingfilm. Spread with half the frosting and top with the second cake. Spread with the remaining frosting and chill until ready to serve. Serve scattered with edible flowers, if liked.

500 g (1 lb 2 oz) carrots
100 g (3½ oz) soft dried pineapple
1 teaspoon ground ginger
¼ teaspoon ground allspice
150 g (5 oz) dried figs, stalks
    removed
75 g (3 oz) golden raisins
150 g (5 oz) medium oatmeal
edible flowers, to decorate
    (optional)

**Lime cashew frosting**
150 g (5 oz) cashew nuts
75 ml (3 fl oz) almond milk
50 ml (2 fl oz) maple syrup
finely grated zest of 1 lime, plus
    3 teaspoons juice

Serves **10**
Prep time **20 minutes, plus
   chilling and soaking**

# RAW CHERRY & ALMOND CAKE
## with Chocolate Ganache

200 g (7 oz) almonds
50 g (2 oz) cacao butter
1 teaspoon almond extract
75 g (3 oz) coconut flour
3 tablespoons coconut palm sugar
300 g (10 oz) fresh cherries, pitted
   and chopped, plus extra to
   decorate

**Ganache**
225 g (8 oz) coconut oil
175 g (6 oz) cacao powder
225 ml (7½ oz) agave syrup

Serves **10**
Prep time **25 minutes,**
   **plus soaking and chilling**

AFFORDABILITY
1

**1** Put the almonds in a bowl, cover with cold water and let soak for several hours or overnight.

**2** Line 2 × 15 cm (6 inch) round cake tins with clingfilm.

**3** To make the ganache, put the coconut oil in a small heatproof bowl and stand it in a larger heatproof bowl of boiling water. Let melt. Pour into a food processor, add the cacao powder and agave syrup and process until thick and glossy. Transfer to a clean heatproof bowl and set aside.

**4** Put the cacao butter in a small heatproof bowl and stand it in a larger heatproof bowl of boiling water. Let melt.

**5** Thoroughly drain the nuts, then transfer to the food processor (there's no need to clean it). Add 4 tablespoons of the chocolate ganache, the almond extract, coconut flour, coconut palm sugar and melted cacao butter. Process until combined. Remove the blade from the processor and stir in the chopped cherries.

**6** Divide between the prepared tins and press down firmly. Chill for at least 3 hours.

**7** Carefully turn one of the cakes out on to a flat serving plate and peel away the clingfilm. Spread with a third of the ganache mixture. (If the ganache has solidified, stand the bowl in a larger heatproof bowl of boiling water and leave until softened, stirring frequently.) Position the second cake on top and spread the top and sides with the remaining ganache. Serve decorated with extra cherries.

# BANANA & STRAWBERRY
## *ice cream*

525 g (1 lb 3 oz) carton vanilla
  soya custard
250 ml (8 fl oz) soya cream
3 bananas, roughly chopped
175 g (6 oz) hulled strawberries
3 tablespoons maple syrup

Serves **6**
Prep time **30 minutes, plus
  freezing**

1 Blend the custard, cream, bananas, half the strawberries and the maple syrup together in a blender or food processor until smooth.

2 Pour the mixture into a freezerproof container and freeze for 3 hours until just starting to freeze around the edges.

3 Scrape the mixture into a bowl and beat with a stick blender or spatula until smooth.

4 Finely chop the remaining strawberries, stir into the mixture and return to the container. Freeze for 3-4 hours or overnight until firm. Allow to soften for 15 minutes before serving.

AFFORDABILITY
**1**

## STUDENT TIP

**FAT CAN BE FRIENDLY** This is especially true for vegans: don't be fooled by low-fat versions of non-dairy milk, yogurt and cheese. The fat is often replaced by low-nutritious alternatives and your body needs a certain amount of 'healthy' fats for energy.

# Raspberry, Pistachio & Rose
# SEMIFREDDO

1 Put the pistachios in a bowl, cover with cold water and let soak for several hours or overnight.

2 Line a small 600 ml (1 pint) loaf tin or similar-size freezerproof container with clingfilm.

3 Coarsely mash the raspberries with a fork. Drain the nuts, then coarsely chop.

4 Scrape off the top thick layer of coconut cream into a bowl. Discard 1 tablespoon of the water left in the can, then add the remaining water to the bowl. Beat with a spoon until thickened and softly peaking. Beat in the agave syrup and rose extract.

5 Gently stir in the pistachios and raspberries and tip the mixture into the prepared tin. Spread the surface level and freeze for at least 4 hours or overnight until firmed up.

6 If frozen overnight, transfer the semifreddo to the refrigerator about 1 hour before serving. Invert onto a plate or board and peel away the clingfilm. Cut into slices and serve scattered with extra raspberries.

75 g (3 oz) shelled pistachios
150 g (5 oz) raspberries, plus extra to serve
320 g (11½ oz) coconut cream, chilled overnight
3 tablespoons agave syrup
1 teaspoon rose extract

Makes **6**
Prep time **10 minutes, plus overnight soaking, chilling, and freezing**

# *Watermelon* SORBET

1.5 kg (3 lb) sweet red watermelon
  flesh, deseeded
juice of 1 orange
zest of ½ orange
1 cm (½ inch) piece of fresh root
  ginger, peeled and thinly sliced

Serves **4-6**
Prep time **10 minutes,
  plus freezing**

**1** Chop the watermelon into cubes and place with the orange juice, orange zest and ginger in a food processor or blender. Process for 1-2 minutes until smooth.

**2** Pour the mixture into a freezerproof container and freeze for 1½ hours, or until half-frozen. Take the mixture out of the freezer and whisk. Return to the container. Whisk at least twice more during the freezing time. There should be plenty of air whipped into the sorbet or it will be too icy and hard. Cover and freeze completely.

**VARIATION**
For cantaloupe & lychee sorbet, replace the watermelon with 1 ripe medium-size cantaloupe, peeled, deseeded and cut into 2.5 cm (1 inch) pieces. Replace the orange juice and zest with juice and zest from ½ a lime. Process the cantaloupe in a mixer for 2-3 minutes, or until smooth. Add the flesh from 550 g (1 lb 4 oz) canned lychees (reserve the syrup) and give a few more pulses, then pour the mixture into a bowl. Warm the lychee syrup with 1 cm (½ inch) piece of fresh root ginger, finely grated, for 2-3 minutes. Allow to cool before adding it to the cantaloupe and lychee mixture. Whisk twice during freezing.

AFFORDABILITY

**1**

# APPLE, PEACH & STRAWBERRY LOLLIES

1  Halve the peaches, remove the stones, roughly chop the flesh and juice in a blender or food processor.

2  Add one-third of the water and spoon the mixture into 3-4 lolly moulds. Freeze until just set.

3  Roughly chop the apple and juice in a blender or food processor. Add one-third of the water and pour over the frozen peach mixture. Freeze until just set.

4  Hull the strawberries, then juice them in a blender or food processor. Add the remainder of the water, pour over the frozen apple mixture and freeze until set.

**VARIATION**
For orange & strawberry juice, hull 200 g (7 oz) strawberries and juice them with 2 oranges.

2 peaches
300 ml (½ pint) water
1 red apple
125 g (4 oz) strawberries

Makes **3-4**
Prep time **10 minutes, plus freezing**

AFFORDABILITY
1

# BACK TO BASICS

SALAD DRESSING

PANCAKES

VEGETABLE STOCK

# PANCAKES

250 g (8 oz) self-raising
wholemeal flour
pinch of salt
500 ml (18 fl oz) rice milk or soya
milk
1 tablespoon lime juice
rapeseed oil, for frying

Serves **4**
Prep time **5 minutes**
Cooking time **10 minutes**

1 Mix the flour and salt with the milk and lime juice and beat together to make a smooth batter.

2 Heat a heavy nonstick frying pan until very hot, then pour in a dribble of rapeseed oil and swirl it round the pan.

3 Add just enough pancake mix to barely cover the bottom of the pan in a thin, even layer. Cook for about a minute, until the bottom has set and become lightly browned, then flip the pancake over and cook the other side.

4 Serve the pancakes hot, spread with vegan cream cheese and jam or maple syrup. If you prefer a savoury breakfast, top the pancakes with the cream cheese plus yeast extract and gherkins.

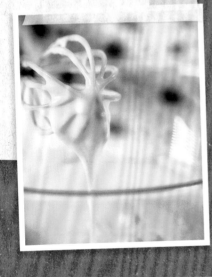

AFFORDABILITY
1

# Salad DRESSING

4 tablespoons pumpkin seed oil
  or hempseed oil
1 tablespoon flax oil
2 teaspoons vegan Dijon mustard
1 tablespoon balsamic vinegar
salt and pepper

Serves **4**
Prep time **5 minutes**

1 Mix all the ingredients together and use as required. The dressing will keep for 1 week in the refrigerator.

AFFORDABILITY
1

# SOYANNAISE

1. Put the soya milk and salt in a saucepan and heat until hot, but not boiling.

2. While whisking the milk with a hand-held blender, add the oil and vinegar.

3. Still whisking, add the crushed garlic, if using, mustard and flax oil. Refrigerate and use as required. It will keep for up to 1 week.

125 ml (4 fl oz) soya milk
pinch of salt
100 ml (3½ fl oz) sunflower oil
2 teaspoons vegan white wine
 vinegar
1 garlic clove, crushed (optional)
1 tablespoon vegan Dijon mustard
25 ml (1 fl oz) flax oil

Serves **4**
Prep time **5-10 minutes**
Cooking time **2 minutes**

# VEGETABLE
## *Stock*

1 Put all the ingredients into a large saucepan. Bring to the boil and simmer gently for 30 minutes, skimming when necessary.

2 Strain the stock, cool then refrigerate it. It will keep for up to a week in the refrigerator, or up to 3 months in the freezer.

500 g (1 lb 2 oz) mixed vegetables, excluding potatoes, parsnips, or other starchy root vegetables, chopped
1 garlic clove
6 peppercorns
1 bouquet garni
1.2 litres (2 pints) water

Makes **1 litre (1¾ pints)**
Prep time **5-10 minutes**
Cooking time **35 minutes**

# INDEX

# Acknowledgements

**Dreamstime.com**  Ahidden 23 above left; Alexey Stiop 55 above left; Andrey Maslakov 86; Baibaz 87 below; Brad Calkins 123 right; Cleardesign 54; Dpimborough 123 left; Jabiru 55 below; Lightfieldstudiosprod 22; Lisa870 122; Makik 87 above left; Martinmark 23 below right; Monkey Business Images 138; Mustipan 55 above right; Raluca Tudor 139 above; Richard Griffin 87 above right; Svetlana Kolpakova 139 below; Tommaso79 23 above right; Vadymvdrobot 160.

**iStock**  Geber86 161 above; GMVozd 216; redhumv 214; SolisImages 161 below; sunara 219; sykkel 217.

**Octopus Publishing Group**  Clive Bozzard-Hill 45, 47, 66, 99, 100, 121, 134, 151, 178, 180; Eleanor Skan 119, 127, 212; Gus Filgate 88; Ian Wallace 64; Lis Parsons 10, 11, 13, 15, 48, 53, 59, 68, 133, 187, 192, 194, 198, 199, 203, 204, 205, 206, 207, 209, 211, 213; Neil Mersh 52; Sandra Lane 193; Stephen Conroy 39, 82, 106, 128; Will Heap 34, 51, 56, 57, 61, 65, 73, 79, 80, 81, 85, 112, 125, 129, 131, 140, 189, 190, 195; William Reavell 37; William Shaw 14, 17, 19, 21, 25, 26, 27, 28, 33, 36, 38, 40, 41, 43, 49, 50, 60, 62, 63, 67, 69, 70, 71, 83, 84, 89, 91, 92, 93, 101, 102, 104, 107, 109, 111, 115, 117, 118, 137, 142, 147, 149, 153, 157, 162, 169, 170, 171, 173, 174, 175, 177, 179, 183, 188, 196, 197, 201, 202.

**Publisher** Sarah Ford
**Extra recipes by** Joanna Farrow
**Features writer** Cara Frost-Sharratt
**Junior Editor** Ella Parsons
**Copy Editor** Francesca Ryan
**Senior Designer** Jaz Bahra
**Designer** Jeremy Tilston
**Picture Researcher** Jennifer Veall
**Production Controller** Meskerem Berhane